Castrol

guide to motoring sport

compiled by the staff of
'Motoring News' and
'Motor Sport'

edited by Jeremy Walton

Patrick Stephens, London

PSL

796.720942

First published—October 1971.

ISBN 0 85059 078 7.

Text set in 9 on 10 pt
Times Roman. Printed on
Brochure Printing 100 gm² and
bound in Great Britain for
Patrick Stephens Limited,
9 Ely Place, London EC1N 6SQ,
by Blackfriars Press Limited,
Leicester LE5 4BS.

Contents

Introduction

MOTORING SPORT is a complicated and colourful sport. This book has been designed and written by a team of experts who either provide the background support needed for there to be any racing at all, or who spend much of their time reporting on the latest developments of interest to enthusiasts. We all felt that this rapidly growing sport—it is now estimated to be the second biggest spectator draw in the United Kingdom—deserved to be better explained to the public who were naturally puzzled by the extraordinary variety of events and cars that can be seen today. Having, we hope, achieved this noble object we then felt it would be a good idea to show where all these activities take place and how to join in.

Unlike many other publications on motoring sport this book sets out to entertain and educate the reader on every facet of the game. Pure track racing is included in detail, but so are such over-the-rough activities as rallying, rallycross and autocross which are often more spectacular as the cars fly from bump to bump. Great events of the past, the 200 mph sports cars, the split second sports such as hillclimbing and drag racing are covered in depth.

The questions most often voiced by the public concerning the sport's rules and the various classifications under which cars race are also explained, together with many superb photographs to illustrate the car categories and catch the high spots of these year-round events. The *Castrol Guide to Motoring Sport* is intended not only to serve as a home reference for those between eight and eighty, but also to take along to the racing, so that the owner need never be baffled by what is taking place around him.

Castrol needs little introduction to anyone, and it was their help and encouragement which enabled this book to be produced by a completely independent editorial team to fill an obvious need. *Motoring News* and *Motor Sport* are both published in London at Standard House, Bonhill Street, the former being a weekly paper covering motor racing and associated activities in depth, whilst *Motor Sport* is an old established monthly motoring journal famous for its forthright manner on all motoring matters, past or present.

Our thanks are due to John Seal and Sally Kemsley of Castrol, and Jenny Martin and Hazel Moseley of *Motoring News* for compiling the appendix data; Tony Matthews for all the drawings in the book; regular *Motoring News* contributors Michael Kettlewell and Peter Noad for the chapters they wrote; and the RAC Motor Sport Division, the RAC Home Touring Division and R. F. A. Edwards of Map Productions Ltd for their helpful assistance.

CHAPTER 1

The origins of motor racing

Those magnificent men in their motoring machines
by W. Boddy

MOTOR RACING is by no means a new sport. In fact, the first great motor
race took place in 1895. It was no milk and water affair either, for it
consisted of a contest from Paris to Bordeaux and back, the primitive
horseless carriages which competed thus being required to cover a
distance of some 732 miles. In spite of this formidable event taking
place in the dark ages of mechanically propelled road vehicles, an entry
of 22 was secured, of which 6 were steam cars, 13 had petrol motors
and Andrè Michelin was using early pneumatic tyres on his Peugeot.
Moreover the first car to complete the return journey, Emile Levassor's
Panhard powered by a twin cylinder Daimler engine of vee formation,
did so in 14 hours 48 minutes, an average speed of 15 mph, only to have
first prize wrested from it and given to Rigoulot's four seater Peugeot.

This cross-country marathon marked the forerunner of many more
races of this stature, such as the 1063-mile Paris-Marseille-Paris race of
1896 (again a Panhard victory with Charron perched high up at the
controls) and the 1350-mile test imposed by racing in the Tour de
France during 1899. Not only did those pioneer races call for courage
and stamina on the part of the racing drivers, but they tested the automobile in its formative years, virtually to destruction in many cases.
Moreover, progress was swift, so that speeds were impressive, to say the
least. Speed hungry car builders installed ever larger engines into crude
wooden chassis frames, refusing to recognise a safety limit for simple
rear-wheel brakes, hard-stressed and equally crude tyres, chain-drive
and steering which had but recently emerged from the era of control
by tiller! In consequence, motor racing at the turn of the century was a
fantastic spectacle for any onlooker who cared to line the public roads
over which it took place. The sight of lofty, noisy, frighteningly powerful machines roaring and rocking across Europe, their heavily-clothed,
begoggled occupants, driver crouching over his wheel, mechanic sitting
on the side-step, as they urged their mechanical steeds onward, ever
onward towards the distant horizon, was enough to excite even ignorant
country peasants. Naturally, spectators were numerous at the road side,
as these giant automobiles, grilled tube radiators at the prow, a pile of
spare tyres strapped on behind, thundered and swayed past, leaving in
their wake a dust cloud as tall as the age old poplars which flanked the
ruler straight French roads. The roads along which the intrepid drivers
—men like Charron, Giradot, de Knyff, Farman, the Renault brothers,
'red devil' Jenatzy, the Englishmen Charles Jarrott and S. F. Edge—
tried to steer. They were halted only if machinery or tyres gave out, the
latter wrenched from the rims at the road side when replacement

became necessary, and by enforced restrictions through towns, when they had to contain their impatience and follow officials riding bicycles.

The pace of these early racing cars was intriguing. At a time before any aeroplane had flown and when a mile a minute was regarded as a good speed from express trains, Levegh's Mors had *averaged* over 40 mph from Paris to Toulouse and back in 1900 and Fournier had won the 1901 Paris to Berlin race, also on a Mors, at better than 44 mph. By 1903 the faster cars, with enormous engines, could approach 100 mph along the straights: Gabriel in a Mors shaped like a boat (the innovation of streamlining) proved able to clock 65.3 mph between Paris and Bordeaux, in spite of seeing little ahead of him but clouds of dust thrown up by slower cars, and having to somehow overtake innumerable other competitors in those hectic, punishing 342 miles.

But it was in this race, intended to run into Madrid from Paris, that disaster struck. The crowds were enormous, riding out to the early morning start on bicycles lit by Chinese lanterns, closing the passage before the cars as they stuttered away on their long journey to a noise akin to the firing of Gatling guns. All down the roads of the continent the spectators crowded the competitors, controlled by a few soldiers. The onlookers were mostly country folk, unaware of the danger they were causing to drivers emerging from the dust clouds at over 90 mph, with scarcely any brakes, on chassis nothing like so 'swervable' as a modern Mini. Naturally, accidents happened. Marcel Renault died, other drivers and onlookers, not to count dogs, were slaughtered. The French Government, horrified, cried halt and those racers which arrived

Large engine, crude chassis: Nazzaro's 1907 Fiat Itala.

Powerful brute: Seaman wrestling with his 1937 Mercedes W125.

in Bordeaux, where the race was stopped, were towed ignominously to the station behind horses.

The nature of this Paris-Madrid (Bordeaux) calamity of 1903 has been exaggerated. It was not in any way so death dealing as the accident at Le Mans in 1955, when Levagh's Mercedes-Benz disintegrated after a collision and mowed down many spectators. But it marked the end, more or less, of open-road, town to town motor racing, which was racing at its fiercest and finest.

The subsequent Gorden Bennett Inter-National races and the Grand Prix, blue riband of such events, which originated in France but were later widely copied, first by Italy in 1923, had by official dictum to be run over closed circuits, although these consisted of public highways shut for the purpose, not special race courses constructed as such. England never permitted even this relaxation, but, in spite of the King's plainly-declared disgust, the 1903 Gordon Bennett race was staged over Northern Irish roads at Athy. Other events, on a lesser scale, were permitted in the Isle of Man, from 1905 onwards and in Ulster, where the sports-car Tourist Trophy found a home from 1928 until another accident involving onlookers killed it by 1936. Even the Channel Islands enjoyed road racing where it survived until the mid 50s as a weekend of speed for holidaymakers.

Generally, however, open road racing died in 1903 and when such roads were used subsequently, they had to be meticulously guarded by police and officials and fenced and bridged where they ran through towns. The cost of this was partially met by charging spectators admission and naturally the problems involved resulted in comparatively short, frequently triangular, courses being used, which the cars lapped many times. Although the circuits thus sanctioned might measure only 14 or 25 miles to a lap, racing continued to be conducted in the Grand Manner. Whereas today's Grand Prix drivers step out, disguised as spacemen with protective helmets, vizors and clothing, from their Formula One projectiles (or mobile fuel tanks)—which are glued to billiard table surfaces by gigantically wide tyres and aerofoils, after a couple of hours or so, before the 1914/18 war a Grand Prix might last a couple of days and cover 700 miles or more! The last one, dominated by Mercedes at Lyon, on the eve of the Kaiser's invasion of Belgium, was over a distance of 467 miles, which Lautenschlager devoured, including corners and depot stops, at an average of 63.35 mph.

But for the non-paying, beside the highway follower of motor racing, the glamour was over—with a few notable exceptions. One of these was the Targa Florio race over a mountainous course in Sicily, first run in 1905, to become a gruelling contest in which the leading drivers sought to outlast one another in Bugatti, Maserati, Alfa Romeo and Mercedes cars. The terrain was so difficult, consisting as it did of rock-strewn roads, suicidal drops over sheer precipices and endless hairpin bends, that overall speeds were relatively low. When Varzi beat Chiron in 1930, his Alfa Romeo did so at 48.48 mph for the 336 miles. The following year the legendary Nuvolari averaged only 40.29 mph to win over the notorious long Madonie course of 363 miles.

With the Tourist Trophy, the Targa Florio is the world's oldest surviving motor race, but the former, ranging from touring car, pure racing car to sports-car contest, has in later years been held at so many different venues, under such changing rules, that its status has suffered badly. The Targa Florio is these days for sports-type cars racing over an abbreviated course which, due to the aforesaid problems and hazards of open road racing, may not survive much longer.

Another late survivor of true town-to-town racing was the sports car Mille Miglia, first held in 1927, which involved racing over normal roads for 1000 miles, from Brescia and back again. This splendid event was won at record speed (97.9 mph) by Stirling Moss' Mercedes-Benz 300SLR in 1955. Alas, it had but a few years to run, for after the Marquis de Portago's Ferrari went into the crowd, causing fatalities in the 1957 race, the Mille Miglia was abandoned.

There are other traditional races which still continue to be held, but all of them are of closed-circuit type. Thus the crowd-drawing 24-hour Le Mans sports car race dating back to 1923, when hooded four-seaters contested it over dusty, stony roads, is still staged but now over a magnificently smooth course. The cars, the course, the times, have changed—witness the 1923 Chenard-Walcker's winning speed of 57.21 mph and 1971's Porsche 917 win at 138.11 mph. Indianapolis, that American track offering a 500 mile dice for specialised single seaters, originated way back in 1911 and posed an insuperable challenge to British cars and drivers between the wars, indeed until Jim Clark in a Lotus-Ford V8 took the Indy winner's flag in 1965, at 150.69 mph. This race, on a track unchanged except in surface material, likewise survives, and is run at ever increasing speeds. America was also the scene of those titanic

CASTROL GUIDE TO MOTORING SPORT

Pan-American races in which the inimitable Fangio learned the art of high speed driving.

But now, the Targa Florio excepted, all the great open-road contests are as dead and buried as hot-tube ignition and the sprag. The casual but enthralled spectator, able to see high-speed motoring by positioning himself or herself at the side of the road, is now confined to European rallies like the Monte Carlo, which, from being a sort of gentleman's tour in 1911 and a he-man's endurance affair in open cars starting from unheard of places in the 1920s, has become quite a thrash.

The interest is as alive as ever. I recall standing in teeming rain in a remote Welsh town to watch a competitors' halt and French mechanics servicing the leading Alpine-Renaults during the 1970 British RAC Rally. Several hundred onlookers were also being soaked to the skin alongside me. Yet here the road sections are run at very sober speeds. How much more exciting for those who strung themselves out along the 10,000 mile route of the London-Sydney Marathon, or the 14,500 miles of the 1970 World Cup Rally, must have found things! The Rally of the Incas also gives something of the thrill and atmosphere of the old road races to the unpaying spectators who watch it.

I hope they, and all you enthusiasts, as you follow such exciting motoring, spare an occasional thought for those pioneer drivers who raced in the inter-town events of long ago, scattering stones, raising dust, with officialdom askance and generations of horses looking at them down their metaphorical noses . . .   □

Brooklands bump: Cobb's Delage leaps away from Eyston.

CHAPTER 2

International competition rules

Who controls the cars you watch—and why
by Mike Cotton

TAKING PART in motor racing is always more fun if you win, and the problem of keeping cars' performances in check has vexed organisers for 70 years. At first there were no rules at all about engine sizes, so the people who built the most powerful cars were usually the most successful. Then handicaps were introduced in an effort to give everyone an equal chance, and incidentally to make the competition more interesting for spectators.

Handicaps are still run today, although they never prove really successful. The rules and handicaps have to be understood by everyone (which isn't often the case) and the best car and driver combination is not necessarily the winner, so handicap events tend not to encourage the best teams.

Minimum car weights and maximum engine sizes have also been tried with success, along with experiments like fuel consumption formulae, but the general way of making racing competitive nowadays is to split categories by engine sizes. In fact the general rules today place a great many restrictions on the designers, and these rules are often difficult to understand even by them, so we had better explain!

Every motor racing country in the world is affiliated to the Federation Internationale de l'Automobile (FIA) in Paris and through its sporting committee, the International Sporting Commission (CSI), every type of car is put into a group where it will meet similar designs on equal terms.

Groups 1 and 2 are for normal production saloon cars, Group 1 for unmodified models and Group 2 for saloons modified within certain limits. Group 3 is for normal production sports cars like the MGB or the Jaguar E type, and Group 4 is for modified sports cars. Groups 5, 6 and 7, as explained in another chapter, are for various types of sports racing cars. Group 8 contains rules for all types of single seater racing cars with separate regulations for Grand Prix cars, Formula 2 and Formula 3. Finally Group 9 is the category for *Formule Libre* cars, which still exist today and race without any restrictions on engine size, minimum weight or dimensions, though they have to comply with the complex safety rules which are laid down.

None of these rules has really altered the original concept that the man who builds the most powerful cars is usually the most successful, and neither does anyone want to prevent that from happening. What it does do is share the winnings among an endless list of categories, for most of the groups are subdivided into a good many cylinder capacity classes. By this means, a designer or driver can decide how much money

Above: Group 2 competition is often very close! Here Brian Muir tries to get from the outside of the track, towards the inside, only to find Frank Gardner's similar 5.7-litre SCA Chevrolet Camaro in the way. Pursuing this battling pair are John Fitzpatrick in the striped Castrol/Broadspeed Escort RS, the similar Fords of Graham Birrell and John Bloomfield, plus Martin Thomas in another Camaro.

Left: Nearest the camera is a classic example of an open Group 6 machine, the French Matra 660, driven by Chris Amon. Overtaking him at Le Mans is Herbert Muller in the Porsche 917.

Below: A selection of Group 4 Prod-sports, showing cars from Jaguar, AC, Marcos, Lotus and British Leyland.

he has to spend, and which category will suit his pocket best. Within a budget, therefore, he can prepare what may be a competitive car and perhaps end a season with an impressive record of class wins, maybe winning a regional championship too.

The spectrum of international motor racing, therefore, goes from a £700 Group 1 Mini or Fiat at one end to a Grand Prix car which, including development costs, might involve an investment of more than £100,000. Most countries have national Formulae using production engines (in Britain, Formula Ford and in France, Formule France using Renault engines). The amateur can race at even less expense by joining the 750 Motor Club and building his own Austin 7 or Reliant powered special for upwards of £300 to drive in British events.

Even the capacity classes themselves are not understood by everyone, so let us look at the basics for a moment. Engine size does not necessarily mean external height and length, but indicates the cylinder capacity. Each cylinder has what is called a swept volume, that is a geometric multiplication of the bore (width of cylinder) by stroke (distance the piston travels up and down on each firing stroke). Roughly speaking, the greater the capacity of each cylinder the greater is the *potential* power of the engine. Note the word potential carefully, for the *actual* power depends just as much on the amount of tuning carried out as on the size of the engine.

In Europe the total of the bore and stroke is measured the French way, in cubic centimetres, but in America and increasingly in other parts of the world the total is in cubic inches. To measure the capacity of an engine, simply multiply the capacity of each cylinder by the

CASTROL GUIDE TO MOTORING SPORT

number of cylinders. An ordinary Austin Mini, for instance, has four cylinders each of 212 cubic centimetres, so the capacity is 848cc. There are 1000 cubic centimetres in one litre, so a 5 litre engine is, alternatively, 5000cc. Incidentally 61 cubic inches are equivalent to one litre, so an American 427 cubic inch V8 engine is, in European language, 7000cc.

Saloon cars in Groups 1 and 2 have the largest number of capacity classes, simply because there are so many different types and makes available to the public. In Britain the lowest capacity class is 850cc which admits Minis, Imps, the Fiat 850 or even a Honda 600 if you wish. The classes put a limit on engine size, but the engine may be smaller, so long as it doesn't fall into a class below. The next class is normally limited to 1000cc cars like the Mini-Cooper, Ford Anglia or the big engined Hillman Imp, and the class above this is usually limited at 1300cc for the Cooper S models, Ford Escort GTs, various Renault models and, a successful model on the Continent, the Alfa Romeo GTA Junior. Stepping up to another class, the next limit is either at 1600cc or 2000cc. The 1600cc limit is more usual, admitting Escort Twin-Cams, BMWs, Alfa Romeos and Hillman Avenger Supers if you like, plus a whole variety of production cars, while the 2000cc class caters for larger capacity Alfa Romeos and BMWs, Escort RS1600 16 valve models and, if you are so inclined, Rover and Triumph 2000s. Usually larger cars compete against each other in the over 2000cc class, which recently has been the domain of American Ford Mustangs and Chevrolet Camaros.

On British tracks you will often see Club Saloons, which do not comply with international rules and which will often be hybrids like

Left: Jean-Pierre Beltoise shows how one takes off in the Matra MS120 Formula 1 car, which conforms to Group 8 of the rules discussed in this chapter.
Below: Group 3 caters for production sports and GT cars with strictly limited modifications, the example we have chosen being the Porsche-VW 914-6 with mid-engine layout.
Right: Group 1 calls for saloon cars closely based on production specification, so all the cars are pretty evenly matched as these Renault Gordinis show!

Escorts with Ford V6 engines installed, or almost any combination of light bodyshell and powerful engine.

Groups 3 and 4, for production and modified sports cars, have fewer limits. The first one normally is at 1000cc and the second at 1150cc, both featuring Sprites, Midgets and Spitfires mainly but also including Lotus Sevens, Ginettas and small production models with Ford, BMC or Triumph engines. The 1600cc class includes Marcos (with Ford's 1600cc engine), Lotus Elans and Lotus Sevens. In the 3 litre class there is usually a straight battle between the Austin-Healey 3000 and the MGC along with the TVR Tuscan V6, while the over 3000cc class is generally a benefit for Jaguar E types and Tridents with 4.7 litre V8 engines.

All these saloon and sports car categories are popular among spectators, who can identify the cars they buy and drive themselves. Often the enjoyment is increased when a small capacity car like a Sprite or a Mini can take on much more powerful cars, like Jaguars, because the smaller cars are more nimble on difficult circuits.

In Groups 5, 6 and 7 the cars are less easily identified because they are made in much smaller numbers. The categories are defined in the chapter on sports cars, or more accurately sports racing cars. Eligible for Group 5 are homologated models (the process by which cars become approved by the CSI, on behalf of the FIA, for international competition: in this case 25 examples must have been manufactured for sale) including the Ferrari and Porsche 5 litres which reach the top capacity limit, and the Ford GT40. The 2 litre class is a popular one encompassing the Chevron B8 (BMW powered), the same firm's B16 (Ford-Cos-

Far left: Hillclimb cars are often built to Group 9 rules, in which pretty well anything goes, this Chevrolet V8 powered 4-wheel drive Hepworth being a particularly successful example.

Left: Car number 8 is a 3-litre Porsche 908 driven by Tony Dean and conforming to Group 6 rules, but overhauling it are two Group 7 Can-Am machines, Dan Gurney's works McLaren and the controversial Chaparral 'vacuum cleaner' driven by Jackie Stewart.

Above: One of the best of the Group 5 cars was the Ferrari 512M, shown with two wheels just airborne at Nurburgring.

worth FVC powered) and Abarths with Fiat power. Group 6 is for one-off prototypes, and again there is a 2 litre category with its own separate European championship for cars like Abarths, Lola T210 and 212, and Chevron B19. The World Championship for Manufacturers caters from 1972 onwards for the 3 litre models which are made by Ferrari, Porsche, Matra and Alfa Romeo. Virtually anything goes in Group 7, which is for open cars of unlimited capacity including models like the McLaren-Chevrolet, Lola-Chevrolet and Chaparral.

The single-seaters in Group 8 are described fully in another part of this book. The three international single seater Formulae (Formulae 1, 2, and 3) are open to any manufacturer or enthusiast making any car which conforms to the complex regulations regarding engine size, minimum weight, fuel capacity and safety regulations. From 1971 onwards Formula 3 is for single-seaters powered by any homologated (production) 4-cylinder engine of 1600cc capacity, with restrictions on the engine power. F2 in 1972 is for single-seaters with homologated engines of not more than six cylinders and 2-litres capacity. Formula 1 (Grand Prix) is for single-seaters with a free design of engine not exceeding 3-litre capacity, and not more than 12 cylinders. Leading examples are the Ferrari 312B (12 cylinders), the Matra MS120 (12 cylinders), the BRM P160 (12 cylinders) and the Ford-Cosworth V8 powered Brabhams, Lotus, March, McLaren and Tyrrells.

In most categories there are Championships to reward the successful teams, and in Britain the RAC administers the most prestigious championships for the leading sports car driver (Groups 5 and 6) and the leading saloon car driver (Group 2).

CHAPTER 3

Voluntary government

A look at the men who control motoring sport in Britain
by Jeremy Walton

THE NEED for a body of men who decide what can and cannot be done in
any motoring competition is apparent from the first such event one
attends. Who decides how far you must be from the track whilst spectating?
How many cars are allowed to start on a particular track in any one
event? Who decides the way in which cars are built so that the driver may
have an excellent chance of survival after it has left the course in a self-
destructive mood? The answers to these questions, and a thousand others
concerning the running of four-wheel competition in this country, may be
found by travelling to the dignified surroundings of London's Belgrave
Square and entering the busy yet restrained atmosphere at number 31,
for this is the headquarters of the Royal Automobile Club's Motor Sport
Division.

Within its walls a staff of 30 are fully extended in processing the paper-
work needed for the 5000 events which the RAC authorise in Britain every
year, plus all the other office routine involved in running such a complex
sport. The Division also manages to issue over 22,000 competition licences
every year as well, besides being the official motor sporting club in Britain by
virtue of its affiliation to the Federation Internationale de l'Automobile,
(FIA) the governing body respon-
sible for running the sport throughout the world.

Organised competition motoring
was founded in France before the
advent of the twentieth century,
when the legendary Count de Dion
banded together the gentlemen who
had been responsible for successfully promoting the Paris–Bordeaux
road race to form the Automobile
Club de France in 1895. Just two
years later a similar group of in-
fluential British enthusiasts united
to establish the Automobile Club of
Great Britain and Northern Ireland,
a club which later gained royal
recognition to become the RAC.
There was no world central governing body until 1904, when the forerunner of today's FIA was established with a membership com-

*Dean Delamont, director of the Royal
Automobile Club's Motor Sport Division.
Delamont ensures that British opinions
are heard abroad by serving on many
sporting committees.*

posed of the national automobile clubs from each country, the RAC being Great Britain's representative from that date onwards.

The actual regulations under which the sport operates are drawn up by a sub-committee of the FIA known as the Commission Sportive Internationale (CSI), but to further complicate matters each national club draws up its own regulations to govern non-international sport within its country. It is likely, too, that each club will have its own particular interpretation of the CSI's rules when running an international event. However, the system works well in Britain as the RAC control the vast majority of all motoring sport. The notable exceptions to RAC jurisdiction are most stock car racing events and any meeting promoted by a club which is not recognised by the RAC, such recognition being entirely dependent on a motor club voluntarily affiliating itself to the RAC.

With something like 40 years spent in touch with motoring sport on both the organising and participating side, the RAC's sporting department is led by the lively yet retiring Dean Delamont. Physically speaking Delamont is not a big man, but his respectful nickname of 'The Dean' and his smiling composure after many years of hearing the same problems and sometimes abuse presented to his institution, suggest there's a lot of determined spirit packed into his neat appearance.

As the body which represents motoring competition law in this country (and it also represents the Government when rally organisers ask for permission to run an event), the RAC Motor Sport Division is often the subject of criticism, yet it is entirely self financing and there is no other body which looks remotely well enough equipped to do the same job. With regulations as complicated as they are today, and greater public concern over noise levels, any governing body would have its work cut out to please all of the people all of the time, especially as top flight motor sport is increasingly supported by big business concerns who naturally wish to make the most of the money they have invested.

Talking to Delamont in his office, appropriately numbered 10 in view of his role as the 'Prime Minister' of the sport, allowed the author to appreciate how much the United Kingdom owes to the enthusiastic clubs who have built up all the facets of British motoring competition to the point where foreign drivers come here to learn their craft.

Before the second World War the RAC was running the British Grand Prix, the Tourist Trophy for sports cars and the RAC Rally, all with the help of a Competitions Committee, a body which still exists today. After the war the RAC led the revival of international circuit racing in the United Kingdom, staging the October 1948 Grand Prix at Silverstone. By 1951 it was felt that the ruling body of the sport should not run a race circuit, so Silverstone was handed over to the British Racing Drivers Club (BRDC). The latter club, plus the British Automobile Racing Club (BARC) and the British Racing and Sports Car Club (BRSCC), are still the leading motor racing clubs today. For the RAC the biggest change came with the formation in 1964 of the Motor Sport Division at Belgrave Square, the parent club staying on at its august headquarters in Pall Mall. Also in 1964 the British Government were forced by public demand to establish some control over rallying, a task with which the then new sporting department was entrusted.

Even with the Government regulations and difficulties with residents who are annoyed by rallies passing within earshot, Delamont commented

Chain of command for the organisation of a typical race meeting

that it was rallying which really formed the backbone of British motor sport. 'In fact', Delamont said, 'there was a 19 per cent increase in the number of rally competition licences issued in 1971, compared to approximately 2 per cent more circuit racing licences, so we consider that this side of the sport is faring exceptionally well'. Apart from circuit racing and rallying, the division is also responsible for the legislation applying to karting, all speed events (autocross, sprints, autotests, rallycross, sand racing) and sporting trials. Every year the RAC Motor Sport Year Book and Fixture List (commonly known as 'the blue book' because that is the colour of its covers) is published: in 1971 this book covered 328 pages listing all the rules pertaining to the sport, as well as sections devoted to circuit diagrams, motor club addresses and a complete list of all competitions scheduled for the forthcoming year. Truly it can be said that nobody who is any way concerned with motor sport can be without a blue book, which is normally published in January of each year. All those who purchase competition licences automatically receive a blue book, as well as *RAC Motor Sport News*, a newspaper now produced every other month to inform 34,000 recipients of any policy or regulation changes since the publication of the blue book. Because this newsheet is only produced on alternate months any important announcements in between times are advertised in *Motoring News*.

To keep everyone fully informed during a year the department spends £10,000 just on postal charges! To regain the money expended on items such as that, the Club has to make a profit on its charges for various obligatory forms, permits to run events, registration fees for affiliated clubs, the use of special stages for rallies, course inspection fees, officials' expenses, record certificate fees for British runs and all the publications which are available from Belgrave Square. By far the greatest amount of money earned by the sporting department comes from competition licences, which account for 60 per cent of all income and include the £30 entrant's licence needed by commercial companies.

Backing up Delamont in his role of director is his deputy Basil Tye who inspects circuits for safety, enforces discipline where needed and keeps a close eye on motor sport 'politics' within the United Kingdom, whilst Delamont looks after the same subject abroad. Responsible in turn to Tye on an equal basis are three men: Christopher Belton, Neil Eason Gibson and Les Needham. In order, their chief tasks are the authorisation of rallies, the promotion of RAC motor sport and overseas authorisation. Belton is the youngest of the trio. A former serviceman, he told us that of the 5000 competition permits issued every year approximately 240 are for race meetings, 250 for sprints and hillclimbs, 400 sanction auto-

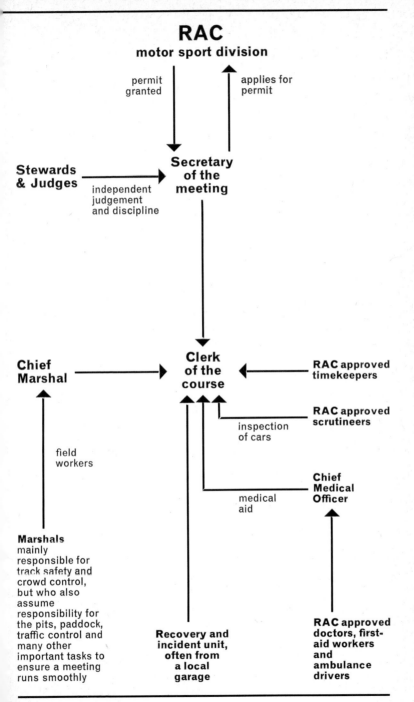

RAC
motor sport division

permit granted

applies for permit

Stewards & Judges

independent judgement and discipline

Secretary of the meeting

Chief Marshal

Clerk of the course

RAC approved timekeepers

RAC approved scrutineers

inspection of cars

field workers

Chief Medical Officer

medical aid

Marshals mainly responsible for track safety and crowd control, but who also assume responsibility for the pits, paddock, traffic control and many other important tasks to ensure a meeting runs smoothly

Recovery and incident unit, often from a local garage

RAC approved doctors, first-aid workers and ambulance drivers

crosses, while the rest of the authorisations go to the rallying fraternity and smaller events which do not fall readily under any heading. Every year the rallying department receives something like 1500 applications to run events, but only recently have more than half of these hopeful organisers received permits. Eason Gibson is a worthy successor to his racing father, coming to the RAC via the BRDC, whilst Needham was formerly a British Leyland Competitions employee.

Looking at the Ordnance Survey maps of popular rallying areas, especially one of the Welsh maps, we could see why there is only a 50 per cent success rate in obtaining permission to run a rally. The trouble is that too many enthusiasts know the best rallying country and all of them want to use it. Bearing in mind the Government's instruction that no more than 'a tolerable level of nuisance' be caused to local residents, the RAC ensure that rallying in popular country is only active at well separated intervals.

In our interviews at the RAC it was stressed again and again that no branch of motor sport can survive without the vast voluntary army of officials and marshals who are needed to run the events. As an example Dean Delamont pointed out that at the British Grand Prix no less than 600 of these unpaid workers are needed to ensure both the safety and efficiency of Britain's contribution to the World Championship of Drivers, and that figure leaves out the officials who actually control the meeting! To simplify the situation we have drawn up a chart which shows the personnel needed to run a race meeting, with their duties. Just how many people are required will depend on the size and nature of the event. As an example of this variation in numbers we found that whereas a small meeting may have just 2 doctors, the British GP boasts 47 such qualified medical men, backed up by no less than 200 first aid workers. In all probability the only qualified members of that 'army', apart from the medical personnel, will be the RAC recognised scrutineers who conduct the technical inspection of competitors' cars, and the timekeepers.

If you want to become a part of this hardy band who get their satisfaction from braving all weathers to ensure that others enjoy their sport, then join a local motor club and enlist! Sometimes you will get the best view that it is possible to get of the competitors (courage is a desirable quality in any marshal!) but most of all you will meet fellow enthusiasts and often learn a number of new skills in to the bargain. *The* marshals' organisation is the British Motor Racing Marshals' Club (BMRMC), which was founded in 1957 to provide a central source of supply of experienced officials and marshals.

For a look into the future of motoring competitions in this country we go back to Dean Delamont. 'Apart from an increasingly professional attitude, I don't see that much will change basically in the next 20 years even though the cars and people will be new', he said and continued with his often repeated sentiments, 'what we in the RAC have to do is ensure that an inexpensive way of participating is always open; simplify the bewildering number of formulae; and, above all, maintain and improve the standard of the sport in both safety and good relations with the public.'

In 20 years time motor sport could well be the British public's favourite spectator sport (it is popularly estimated to be around halfway up the 'top ten' of viewing sports now) and with that growth the RAC Motor Sport Division will face its sternest challenge yet: there will be no room for anything but the professional approach then! ☐

CHAPTER 4

Formula 1

What makes the big wheels tick?
by Andrew Marriott

JACKIE STEWART sits motionless swathed in his flameproof overalls; if you could see his face, which is encased in an all-enveloping helmet, it would show little emotion except a dedicated determination to win. All around there is a cacophony of sound from other racing cars. This is the grid one minute before the start of a World Championship Grand Prix. Stewart's Tyrrell is a vivid blue machine, the object of devoted attention from a dedicated band of mechanics who have, more than likely, slaved away half the night. The car is really little more than carefully formed sheets of aircraft-type aluminium built into the tube-like shape of the Tyrrell. Without fuel, it weighs only a fraction more than 1000 lb, almost half that of a Cortina 1600. But the Cosworth V8 engine that is now revving to almost 10,000 rpm gives somewhere in the region of 450 brake horsepower. That is equivalent to about eight Cortina engines! Every part in that engine has been built from the finest materials, worked by craftsmen, checked and double checked. It cost £7500 to buy and needs to be taken apart and rebuilt with new parts between races.

The flag drops and Stewart makes the best start from the pole position. The vast roller-like rear tyres, each more than a foot wide, bite

---

The leading driver and car for much of 1971 was Jackie Stewart and his Cosworth V8 powered Tyrrell, shown here with revised nose-cone.

into the tarmac. The immense power from the engine spins the wheels and the rubber almost boils as it claws for grip. The race is on and for the next hour and a half the 20 or so drivers, all in similar ultra-powerful, lightweight cars, will be fighting to get to the chequered flag first. Their neck muscles will become strained while they combat the G forces that are produced as the fantastic adhesion of the best tyres and suspensions in the world keeps the cars glued to the road at a speed which would long since have sent even the best handling Mini sliding wildly out of control. The specially made ventilated disc brakes will glow red hot from the strain of slowing the cars time and again from 160 mph to a near standstill. For some of them it will all be too much and the machine will grind to a halt. It is just as likely that the fault might be something like a broken rotor arm in the distributor or a suspension part which could no longer stand the strain. Far less likely is a retirement due to a crash, for these are the top drivers in the world and their control of the situation when something goes wrong is computer-like. But things can go wrong, and when they do everything happens very quickly. Often it is in the lap of the gods whether the driver steps out unscathed or suffers injury, or worse. That is why he takes every precaution, like wearing special fireproof clothing, and being strapped firmly into his car, while the machine itself has many built-in safety features, such as special fuel cells, fire extinguisher systems and so on.

Suddenly it is the last lap and Stewart roars across the line to take the spoils of victory and possibly as much as £25,000 in prize money. But it is not a victory for just one man. Behind him were the mechanics, the designer of the car, the team manager who made sure everything went according to plan, the tyre technicians who now play such an important role, and back at the factory the men that built the engine. A real team effort.

This then is Formula 1 racing, to the great majority of fans the premier category of motor racing. It is the goal for which every aspiring driver aims. Few make it, and when they do only one man can win the World Championship, contested over those dozen or so races held in countries in Europe and America. Some people may argue that the Can-Am cars, those big sports racing machines with their 8-litre Chevrolet engines which compete on the North American continent, are faster than Formula 1. Perhaps they are, but the competition at the top is not nearly as tough. Others will contend that the turbocharged Indianapolis cars are faster. Of that there is no doubt, but they are built for special oval racing circuits and certainly do not handle as well. For all round performance and hot competition there is no doubt that Formula 1 leads the way.

The Formula 1 World Championship was started back in 1950 but, of course, there was Grand Prix racing long before that. The first Grand Prix was held at Le Mans in France in 1906 and was battled out between the normal road cars of that day. Soon Grand Prix racing was catching on in other countries and the cars were quickly developing into 'specials' just for racing, regulations being laid down to govern the size of the engines and other technical features.

After the first world war, Grand Prix racing became firmly established in several countries and continued to grow in stature. Soon the racers were becoming known as 'Grand Prix' cars, although the formula

1971 Tyrrell-Ford Formula 1 car

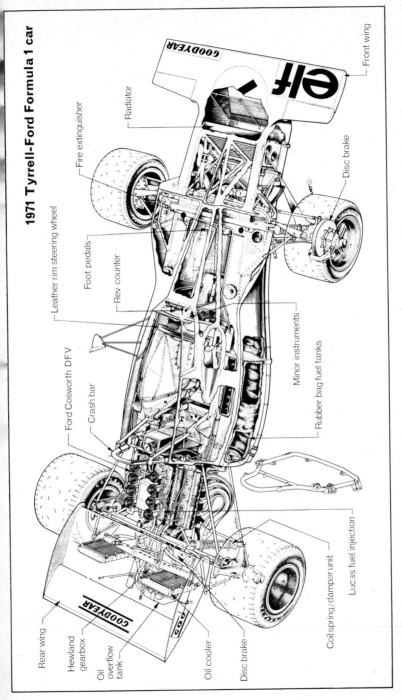

Front wing

Radiator

Fire extinguisher

Disc brake

Leather rim steering wheel

Foot pedals

Rev counter

Minor instruments

Ford Cosworth DFV

Crash bar

Rubber bag fuel tanks

Lucas fuel injection

Coil spring/damper unit

Disc brake

Oil cooler

Oil overflow tank

Hewland gearbox

Rear wing

was changed from time to time. Britain was rarely in the hunt at that time although briefly, in the 1920s, the Sunbeams and Talbots scored victories.

Probably the most exciting racing cars of all time were produced just before the second world war when the great German Mercedes and Auto Union teams raced for the honour of Nazi Germany, carrying all before them. The cars were breathtakingly powerful, having something like 600 bhp in what are now considered to be very crude chassis. They were huge, the racing was tremendously exciting and particularly thrilled British crowds when they came to the Donington Park circuit near Derby. Many older enthusiasts consider that those days were the best in the history of Grand Prix racing.

By the early 1950s, the works Alfa Romeo, Maserati and Ferrari teams from Italy were making the running and taking all the awards. Then in the mid 1950s Britain became, for the first time, a major contender with victories from the Connaughts and then the Vanwalls. By the end of that decade the face of racing was beginning to change, with the small, privately owned firm of Cooper successfully racing rear-engined cars. Although the Auto Unions of 1938 had been rear-engined (and designed by the same man who designed the Volkswagen) other manufacturers had, up until then, continued to stick to the classic front engined configuration.

By the early 1960s every new Formula 1 racing car was rear-engined and this is still the case today. Another trend was that of the 'special' builder. In previous years the major components for a racing car were all produced by the one firm. Ferrari, for instance, would build not only the chassis but also the engine and gearbox, as did the majority of other manufacturers including Britain's own BRM. Cooper, followed by Lotus and then a crowd of others, just did not have the facilities to develop engines, so they relied on a unit built by the firm of Coventry Climax. This British concern powered many a Lotus and Cooper to victory, continuing to do so until Climax pulled out of racing at the end of 1965.

Two years later the gap they left was filled by the Ford Motor Company, who commissioned a specialist firm, Cosworth Engineering Ltd of Northampton, and its brilliant Chief Engineer Keith Duckworth, to

CASTROL GUIDE TO MOTORING SPORT

Left: McLaren M19, driven by Denis Hulme, who is also a highly accomplished sports car driver.
Above: Bald tyres have become all the rage in Formula 1, as this Ferrari demonstrates!

design an engine capable of bringing back Grand Prix honours to Britain. In the meantime much of the winning had been done by Jack Brabham's team who were using Australian-built Repco engines.

In 1966 new regulations for Formula 1 had been introduced and these allowed the manufacturers to use engines of 3 litres, twice the previous size permitted. Naturally, with more power to play with, the racing was going to become much faster. It was undoubtedly a wise move by the controlling body of motor racing, the FIA in Paris, and the Formula is still in force today and will continue unchanged for some time since it has proved so successful. Times do change, however, and the formulae are revised every so often, more as a spur to the designers than for any other purpose.

The £100,000 that Ford handed over to Cosworth was money well spent. Initially only Lotus had the engines and in fact Jim Clark won the very first time out in a Lotus 49 fitted with the Cosworth engine at the 1967 Dutch GP. Since then Formula 1 machines fitted with these power units have done the great majority of the winning. During the time that it has been in use, horsepower has been increased from 420 bhp to around 460 bhp and over 60 of the engines have been built. Now one can buy them off the shelf for £7500 and, as long as you have a designer and team who can build a decent chassis, you make a Grand Prix car in the space of a few months. Certainly a far cry from 20 years earlier when it took virtually years of hard work to develop a Grand Prix racing car.

Over the past year the Cosworth dominance has tailed off a little and it is good to see that the non 'special' builders are again competitive. Ferrari's flat 12 Formula 1 engine has been an enormous success and the French Matras and British BRMs, both of which use engines of their own manufacture, have had their brighter moments. Alfa Romeo have also come back to Grand Prix racing, although their engines are presently fitted to a chassis of March design, rather than one built by their own company.

At present there are nine manufacturers building and racing Formula 1 cars. The oldest established and currently among the most successful teams is Ferrari. The scarlet red machines are the pride of Italy and are built at Maranello, a little town near Modena. Ferrari builds some of the most sought after and beautiful sports cars in the world: his racing team is an extension of an exceptional mastery of the task of automotive engineering. In fact the giant Fiat motor company now owns Ferrari and thus helps to finance the racing team.

The BRM team, at one time financed by British industry but now owned by the giant engineering group of Rubery Owen, has had its ups and downs since the 1950s. Mainly it has been a story of disappointments with the occasional bright patch. However, during 1971, the team was exceptionally strong with fast drivers, a very good chassis and a powerful and reliable V12 engine built at Bourne in Lincolnshire. For 1970 and 1971 they were sponsored by the Yardley cosmetic company and in return for their financial help the cars were painted in the Yardley colour scheme, the exercise being used as a sales promotion operation. Such sponsorships are becoming more and more a vital part of the Formula 1 scene.

A third firm which produces its own engines and chassis is Matra Sports, the Paris based team which is a department of a French aerospace firm. Matra took over a small sports car manufacturer back in the early sixties, soon got interested in motor racing and by 1965 was building and successfully racing Formula 3 cars. A massive grant from the French government aimed at restoring the country's prestige in racing (Bugatti won many Grands Prix in the 1920s) has proved very successful and Matra, using the considerable resources of its parent company, has been a major name in the sport for five seasons now. After a near miss in 1968, Jackie Stewart (driving a Matra with a British Cosworth V8

Right: Ferrari 312/B2 made its debut at the Brands Hatch Race of Champions.

Below: All-British BRM P160 being skilfully skidded by Mexican Pedro Rodriguez.

Far right: With a front wheel flying over the kerb Jochen Rindt shows the style that made the Lotus 72 a World Champion's car in 1970.

engine) won the World Championship in the following year. Matra have also been developing their own V12 engines which, after some troublesome times, are now showing more promise. Needless to say, in the wake of Matra victories has grown a new generation of very talented French drivers.

The remaining six constructors all use Ford Cosworth V8 engines in the back of their cars. In every case the engine acts as part of the chassis, taking all the stresses and strains. The engine is bolted to the rear of the monocoque chassis just behind the driver's seat. At the back of the engine is the special five speed racing gearbox supplied by Hewland Engineering who, due to their many successes through the years, virtually have a monopoly. Supported on the gearbox is a bridge on to which hangs the rear suspension. There is no other connection between this and the back of the monocoque, thus the engine is literally part of the chassis: a very clever idea, pioneered by Colin Chapman of Lotus, which saves weight apart from having several other important advantages.

Of the six manufacturers using Cosworth engines, three of them—March, Tyrrell and Surtees—have been building Grand Prix racing cars for less than two years. March, run by a lawyer, a designer and a team manager, is a firm which was only announced in September 1969 and yet, by 1970, had two top drivers in its own Formula 1 team and had made and sold cars to other entrants for Mario Andretti and Jackie Stewart to drive. In the early part of that season the cars did fantastically well, but since then their Formula 1 fortunes have slipped somewhat, although in other racing categories March cars are high in the results.

John Surtees, like Bruce McLaren and Jack Brabham before him, was a driver who felt he could get together a team to build a better car than the one he was already driving. At first his cars were for Formula 5000 racing but now he has built his own Formula 1 car, which first appeared at the 1970 British GP.

Ken Tyrrell was himself a racing driver for some time but later he realised his talents lay in team management rather than driving. He ran works Formula 2 and 3 Coopers and in 1964 signed up a young Scottish driver called Jackie Stewart. Shortly after, Tyrrell became connected

with Matra and ran an F2 car for Stewart and later Matra Formula 1s also for the Scot. Then he became a customer for a March in 1970, but soon after decided to become a constructor in his own right. The Tyrrell-Ford was one of motor racing's best kept secrets and when it first appeared in August 1970 it was quite obviously very competitive even if it was perhaps a little like the Matra. Tyrrell's dedicated team took some time to sort the car fully but Stewart took the machine to its first win in the 1971 Spanish GP. Tyrrell has neither the facilities nor the inclination to produce his racing cars for sale to other entrants or drivers.

Lotus, like Ferrari, rely for their main source of income on building exciting road-going sports cars, at their factory near Norwich. But it all started from Colin Chapman's love of motor racing. The Lotus chairman still spends a great deal of his time working on racing projects and though now also a big business man he still finds time to design some of the world's most advanced racing cars. In the hands of the late Jim Clark, the late Jochen Rindt and Graham Hill, Lotus have achieved great success and won the Formula 1 Constructors' Championship four times. Their present car, the Lotus 72, has a novel torsion bar suspension system and it was with this exciting wedge shaped design that Rindt won the 1970 Championship. Colin Chapman has always been an innovator and many of the ideas which he developed, such as the monocoque chassis, later became the standard which others followed.

Jack Brabham and Bruce McLaren both left the ailing firm of Cooper and set up as racing car constructors in their own right. Both have been successful, and though Jack has now retired and Bruce was tragically killed while testing at Goodwood in 1970, both of their companies continue. Brabham's firm (now run by his Australian partner and designer Ron Tauranac) won the World Championship in 1966 and 1967 and are renowned for building well engineered cars which are relatively easy to drive, thus they have sold a great number of racing cars for the lesser formulae.

The McLaren team's main successes have been in the Can-Am Championship which they have dominated since 1967, but they still

28

build fine Formula 1 cars at their Colnbrook, Buckinghamshire factory.

It would be nice to see some of the other major world motor manufacturers back in Formula 1 such as Mercedes, British Leyland and so on. This is unlikely at present although there is always a possibility that both Honda and Porsche may return to Formula 1.

It is always difficult to predict the future accurately, and quite what the Grand Prix car of 1980 will look like is impossible to determine. In 1969 it looked as if four wheel drive might be the answer and several manufacturers, even the Cosworth engine concern, built and tested cars, but so far they have not proved successful. Another possibility has been the use of gas turbine engines and Lotus currently have such a car for evaluation. Again turbine power is difficult for the driver to control and (after the initial excitement) can be rather boring for the spectators since the turbine makes very little noise. By 1980 the Wankel rotary engine may well be more firmly established and possibly have a big hold on racing. We will just have to wait and see.

One thing is certain, tens of thousands of racing drivers all over the world will continue to drive for all they are worth in an attempt to win one of those few coveted places at the top of the motor racing tree— a Formula 1 drive.

Left. Formula 1 car of the future? Dave Walker in the 4-WD Lotus turbine 56B leads Gijs van Lennep's Surtees TS7 and Siffert's shovel-nosed BRM P160.
Above: Graham Hill's Brabham BT34 'lobster claw' with Cosworth V8 leads Chris Amon's Matra.
Right: Swift Swedish driver Ronnie Peterson shows off the March 711's aerodynamically inspired lines.

CHAPTER 5

The breeding formulae

A look into the single seaters in which tomorrow's stars
learn their craft
by Alan Henry

THE ULTIMATE ambition of many professional racing drivers is a place in a
Formula 1 team and the chance of having a crack at the World Championship. So there has always been tremendous competition to star in the
classes immediately below Formula 1. Such is the highly competitive
nature of the sport that only a few who aspire to a Formula 1 position will
win a Grand Prix, let alone a championship, but to drive in a Grand Prix
at all is a commendable achievement, for to have done so generally reflects
success in either Formula 2 or Formula 3 classes in which the racing is as
fierce as in Formula 1 itself, with dozens of hopefuls striving to the limit
of their abilities (and sometimes beyond!) to catch the discriminating eye
of a top team manager.

Not all Grand Prix stars come up through single seater racing. German
ace Rolf Stommelen, who drove the works F1 Surtees during 1971, made
his name with Porsche sports cars, having some tremendous races in the
Porsche 917 coupé which was *more* powerful than the F1 car he currently
drives. While it didn't teach Stommelen anything about open wheel racing,

Left: Jochen Rindt shows the verve that made him 'king' of Formula 2, sliding his Lotus 69 ahead of Clay Regazzoni in the Tecno and Jackie Stewart's Brabham at Crystal Palace in London. Above: A typical Formula 2 bunch led by Ronnie Peterson in the March 712M, pursued by Francois Cevert's Tecno.

it taught him how to handle power, and he was driving in his first Grand Prix less than a year after his first single seater outing.

Generally it's a well-beaten path through F3 and F2, where the new F1 recruit learns his trade. The exceptionally talented can miss out F2 altogether, but not many. Jackie Stewart jumped from his F3 Cooper in 1964 into the number two BRM seat the following year while Emerson Fittipaldi, Brazilian leader of the Lotus team, took his place on a Grand Prix grid less than a year after his first F3 race. The less lucky work away at F3 and F2 for years in the hope that their F1 offer will come: frequently it never does!

Once the bright eyed novice has made his decision that he wants that Grand Prix seat which will be vacant in four years time, then the first step is often Formula Ford. Devised in 1967 as an inexpensive class of single seater racing for the club driver, it immediately opened the door to those who wanted to drive in F3 but were prevented from doing so by the money required to own and maintain this type of car. Therefore FF soon became populated with young professionals who regarded it as the first step on the ladder to a Formula 1 career.

The regulations have remained basically unchanged over four years, demanding the use of Ford Cortina 1600GT motors (on which there is a strict tuning limitation) and their installation in a simple tubular space-frame chassis. The use of readily available road tyres fitted on Cortina-Lotus wheels is another stipulation which keeps costs to a reasonable level and ensures that the novice learns a lot about sliding, spinning, and general car control at relatively low speed. FF racing is always thrilling with plenty of spins and harmless disappearances from the track; all of which has made the class very popular with spectators!

THE BREEDING FORMULAE   31

The first manufacturers of FF cars were Lotus, but many others followed and several new firms also sprang up. The cars use sturdy F3 Hewland gearboxes and generally are extremely reliable, the formula not having suffered from the same cost increases as Formula 3. It's still possible to buy a competitive secondhand race-winning car for around £1000.

There are about a dozen local championships based on individual circuits around Britain as well as a national contest, sponsored in 1971 by the British Oxygen Company. On the continent Formula Ford has caught on, despite the presence of Formula Super Vee, a similar concept using Volkswagen components. A richly sponsored championship is fought out over eight races by leading FF drivers from several countries. The overall prize couldn't be a better endorsement of how highly Formula Ford is thought of as a training ground for F1 talent—it is a test drive in one of Ken Tyrrell's F1 cars under the supervision of this great talent spotter. Notable Tyrrell 'discoveries' were Belgian Jacky Ickx and Jackie Stewart.

Once out of Formula Ford, the next stage up the single seater tree is Formula 3. The cars look substantially the same as FFs, but proper racing engines are admitted, and the latest racing tyres on wide wheels are used. F3 has the advantage of being truly international so that the budding stars from differing countries have an opportunity to compete with each other driving similar cars.

From 1964 to 1970 Formula 3 cars had to use pushrod motors of up to 1000 cc derived from production units, the most popular being the Ford Anglia engine. Look into the history books and you will find a host of names during that period who have later made their mark in Grand Prix racing. Men such as Ronnie Peterson, March's current F1 team leader, Peter Gethin, Emerson Fittipaldi, Reine Wisell, Jack Oliver, Tim Schenken and Howden Ganley: they're all in F1 now.

The formula changed at the start of 1971. Tuning the small one-litre motors had developed into a specialist art and around 120 bhp was being coaxed out of these little 'screamers' by the end of 1970, revving twice as fast as their designers intended some 12 years before! The current Formula 3 uses production motors (the Ford twin-cam, Fiat 124S, Alfa Romeo and BMW 1600 units are allowed) but once again the indications are that Ford will rule the roost. In racing form, a Lotus-Ford Twin Cam develops around 180 bhp when fuel injection is used. In order to reduce the amount of power available the FIA stated that the motor's breathing should be restricted by the use of a 21.5 mm throttling hole through which the air would blow into an airtight chamber before arriving at the motor. This restriction has the effect of cutting power to around 120 bhp and means that they will not rev so highly either. The general idea is to stop prices rising but at present the regulations have not achieved this aim.

The racing is always close. Last lap scrambles to the chequered flag have often resulted in collisions between a number of cars. As many F3 races support Grand Prix events, there is added incentive to shine in front of the top team managers and trade representatives. In 1970 it was generally reckoned that the two races for an F3 driver to win were the Monaco event and the British Grand Prix supporting race. They were won by Tony Trimmer and Mike Beuttler respectively, both of whom have already had their first taste of F1 motoring and seem set for successful careers.

32

Popular proprietary chassis made in Britain include the Lotus 69, Brabham BT35 and the March 713, all very closely related to the Formula 2 cars from the same manufacturers. A new arrival on the British scene is the smart side radiator Ensign (looking rather like a small Lotus 72 F1 car), whilst Renault money has ensured that the French built Alpines are cars which don't rely on Ford power.

So our young driver dutifully wades through Formula 3, completes a season or two with a fair degree of success, including a handful of wins, and looks around for the next move. He may even have won one of the three championships which are organised each year, the Lombank, the Forward Trust and, in its first year the most coveted, the *Motor Sport* Trophy series.

Possibly the most thorough vindication of a young driver's ability is if he proves himself in Formula 2. Hitherto the newcomer's racing will have been against people of his own level, all youngsters anxious for a break, but in F2 he will have the opportunity to pit his ability against established Grand Prix stars driving cars of pretty well the same performance as a 'privateer' can buy.

Right: No, it's not a gun to get rid of pressing rivals! This air-restrictor limits the performance of an F3 engine.
Below: Bev Bond in the Ensign leads David Walker's Lotus during a typical Silverstone Formula 3 race; in 1971 Walker did most of the winning.
Bottom: Tim Schenken was usually in this leading position whilst driving his Formula Ford Merlyn.

The current 1600 cc F2 has been running since the start of 1967 and changes at the end of 1971. The regular winner throughout that period has been the Cosworth FVA motor, although both the Italian Ferraris and German BMWs have had their successful seasons. Factory teams from all major manufacturers have been seen, but there is always a chance for a privateer to buy the equipment used by those teams and stand a fair chance of featuring in the results if he is really good.

Probably the best feature of the formula has been the European F2 Trophy series which enables the newcomers to have their own private contest within the framework of a series of races to which the Grand Prix stars are also admitted. Graded drivers, that is to say drivers who have twice scored world championship points, or who have been classified in the first three overall in a world championship sports car race during the previous two seasons, cannot score points. The points scoring system is on a 9–6–4–3–2–1 basis, similar to the world championship system; if the first two cars in the race are driven by graded drivers, the third man takes maximum European Trophy points.

Formula 2 is a great levelling ground. There's little chance of winning because you've got a greatly superior car, as might arise in Formula 1, although the BMWs and Ferraris were admittedly faster on their day, and the attraction of an F2 race is the possibility of an unknown showing the best drivers in the world the way home! It happened back in 1964, (when there was one-litre F2) as an unknown Austrian called Jochen Rindt beat all the aces to win the London Trophy at Crystal Palace and also later in 1967, when Jacky Ickx pulled out another unexpected win. Both these drivers went right to the top, Rindt in particular ruling F2 for nearly five years until his sad death in 1970—the year in which he became posthumous World Champion. Others to make their name in F2 over the past few years include Jean-Pierre Beltoise, Derek Bell, and the late Piers Courage, while more recently the Swedish pair Ronnie Peterson and Reine Wisell, Scottish driver Gerry Birrell, plus Brazilians Emerson and Wilson Fittipaldi have shown considerable promise.

The cars used in F2 strongly resemble the smaller F3 cars but their construction is sometimes different. Briefly, pure racing cars use either what is called spaceframe or monocoque chassis, the first using lots of small diameter tubes covered by a glassfibre body (very occasionally aluminium is used, especially by Ferrari) and the second being a one piece tub formed of alloy sheeting in most cases—also covered by un-stressed bodywork. The vast majority of F3 cars have spaceframe con-struction (as do Formula Fords) but in F2 either type of manufacture may be found. For example the March firm produce their F2 cars with either tubed spaceframe or monocoque layout. Other popular F2 cars come from Lotus in Norfolk and Brabham in Surrey.

In all the 'breeding formulae', disc brakes and independent suspension are used: it is likely that in the future the use of brakes mounted inboard of the wheel will increase as this move can improve a car's handling and braking.

When you see a field of F2 cars all charging round together you can thank the Ford Motor Company for their foresight in financing Cosworth Engineering to develop the 235 bhp Cosworth FVA engine, based on a Ford cylinder block originally designed for the Lotus Twin Cam engine. Over 90 per cent of F2 cars use this power unit and appropriate Hewland

34

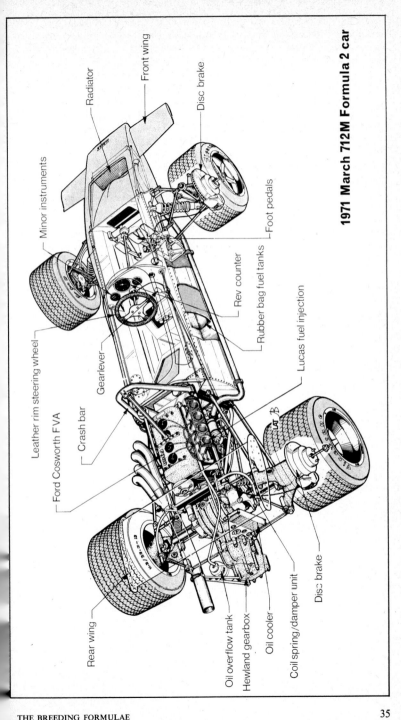

1971 March 712M Formula 2 car

- Front wing
- Radiator
- Disc brake
- Minor instruments
- Foot pedals
- Rev counter
- Rubber bag fuel tanks
- Lucas fuel injection
- Leather rim steering wheel
- Gearlever
- Crash bar
- Ford Cosworth FVA
- Rear wing
- Oil overflow tank
- Hewland gearbox
- Oil cooler
- Coil spring/damper unit
- Disc brake

gearbox with five forward gears to keep the engine on its power band between 7,500 and nearly 10,000 rpm. The exception at present are some of the Italian Tecnos which use another Cosworth engine called the BDA (which can be bought in much more docile form, encased in an Escort!) which is drastically modified by Tecno to give at least as much power as the FVA, but with a wider power band making it easier to drive.

Formula 2 racing is nearly as colourful as F1 and offers closer racing with the stars of tomorrow pitched in against the established men of Graham Hill's or Jackie Stewart's calibre. The opportunities to see F2 in Britain are few and far between so make sure you see some by looking at Forthcoming Events in *Motoring News* or *Motor Sport*.

From F2 upwards progression is in the hands of manufacturers, owners and team managers. One thing is quite certain, of the many who optimistically set out with their sights on a Grand Prix seat, very few will make it. It's been shown that the powerful F5000 cars which use big American V8 motors can provide a stepping stone, but we have yet to see how effective Formula Super Vee turns out to be and also the Formula Atlantic single seater class. From 1972 onwards Formula 2 cars will have larger engines of up to 2-litres, so we can expect this category to be even more spectacular in the future.

Formula 5000: big engines—big future?
by Michael Kettlewell

JOINTLY ANNOUNCED by the British Racing & Sports Car Club and Motor Circuit Developments in mid-1968 for introduction the following year, Formula 5000 is basically a European version of the Sports Car Club of America's Formula A (now also known as Formula 5000). The idea was to introduce a big power category of single seater racing car to supplement Formula 1, but at less cost, and to establish a new rank of international drivers. Indeed, for the first two seasons regular Grand Prix drivers were forbidden to take part in Formula 5000.

From a distance a Formula 5000 car looks similar to a Formula 1 machine: it is big, powerful looking, with an immense engine behind the driver, and sits on huge, wide tyres. In the chassis there is little difference between a Formula 1 or a Formula 5000 machine. All the leading cars are expensive monocoque constructions and, if anything, a Formula 5000 is stronger than its Formula 1 counterpart because it has to cope with a much heavier engine. Instead of a 3-litre thoroughbred power unit designed specifically for racing as in Formula 1, engines for Formula 5000 machines must be 5-litre, eight cylinder Vee layout, mass produced units with pushrod operated valve mechanism. A list of eligible engines includes many American V8s, also the British Rover V8, but in practice it is the Chevrolet Camaro Z28 (originally made for saloon car racing) that reigns supreme. Ford engines have won in the United States, but have never proved successful in Europe.

Engines may be modified, but the cylinder block and the cylinder heads must not be substituted. The location of the camshafts cannot be changed, while the number of main bearings must remain the same. Unlike American rules, fuel injection has been banned since the 1970 season; the Weber 48IDA carburettor is specified for European 5000s. Swiss tuning expert Louis Morand claims 480 bhp for his version of the Chevrolet engine (more than any current Formula 1 engine) but British firms such as Alan Smith of Derby and Charles Lucas Engineering of Huntingdon claim lower maximum power but better torque figures to give more 'punch' out of corners.

Minimum weight limit of a Formula 5000 car is 1250 lb (about half a ton) including oil and water, but not fuel or driver. Few cars get down to that figure owing to the weight of the iron Chevrolet engine. By comparison a Formula 1 car must weigh at least 1168 lb and indeed many are within a few lb of this minimum limit.

To give an idea of costs, a ready to race McLaren M18-Chevrolet similar to that raced by Team Trojan is available at £9070. The chassis costs £5150, the Morand modified Chevrolet is a cool £3500 and the Hewland DG300 five speed racing gearbox costs £420. To allow for maintenance and possible repairs, a team needs a spare engine, a spare gearbox and other parts—such as suspension, body, instruments, tyres, gear ratios, springs, and so on. So to run a Formula 5000 competitively a top team would need to spend at least £13,000 to £15,000, which is an expensive year's motor racing in almost any language!

For the first year of European Formula 5000, which was 1969, Carreras the tobacco company sponsored a series of 12 Guards Championship races, and there were also two non-championship meetings. With a total prize fund of £2500 per meeting, the leading entrants found themselves considerably out of pocket, but were content to treat the season as a try-out for 1970 when a series of 20 races was run, 12 of them with a prize fund of £5000 per race. Significantly, most of the entrants who ran cars in 1969 came back with new machinery for 1970.

The first season got off to a slow start as teams learned about their new cars and, more important, the internals of the 5-litre Chevrolet engine. The organisers anticipated this by admitting 2-litre racing machinery to run concurrently with the Formula 5000s; indeed, some Formula 2 cars have given the Formula 5000s plenty to think about! Peter Gethin in the works backed McLaren M10A with Bartz modified Chevrolet engine dominated the early part of the series, winning at Oulton Park, Brands Hatch (twice) and Mallory Park, before going to

Always among the front F5000 drivers are Frank Gardner (below, left, in the Lola he helped develop) and Brian Redman (below, right) in the Sidney Taylor Team Castrol McLaren. Another front runner is the Surtees (right), here being driven by former World Champion motorcyclist Mike Hailwood.

the United States for some Formula A races. A works Surtees TS5-Chevrolet dominated the early part of the series, winning at Coxyde (Belgium), Zandvoort (Holland), Snetterton and Hockenheim (Germany). Taylor was almost level pegging with Gethin in the championship. The Championship depended on the final round at Brands Hatch where, in a freak accident, both Peter and Trevor were eliminated when lapping a slow backmarker who got in the way, so Gethin won the title by a slender margin. Former motorcycle world champion Mike Hailwood took third place in the series driving the works Lola T142-Chevrolet.

Two up-and-coming drivers were fourth and fifth in the series, Alan Rollinson, who drove both a Formula 2 Brabham BT30-Ford FVA and Doug Hardwick's Lola T142-Chevrolet, and Mike Walker, pilot of Alan McKechnie's Lola T142-Chevrolet. Walker, who won at Silverstone and Oulton Park, was given the premier Grovewood Award at the end of the year, being voted by a panel of motoring journalists as the most promising up-and-coming driver of 1969.

For 1970 two new marques joined the established McLaren, Lola and Surtees makes; they were Lotus and Leda. Neither were to prove very successful and it was 1969 all over again with Peter Gethin winning the Guards title for the second year running. Driving Sid Taylor's works-supported McLaren M10B-Chevrolet, Gethin won eight races and scored three second places from 13 starts. By the middle of the year he had won a place in the McLaren Formula 1 and Can-Am teams, but still no one could surpass his total of points! New Zealander Howden Ganley took second place with one victory, five seconds and six thirds. Ganley drove a second works assisted McLaren M10B-Chevrolet, this one backed by Barrie Newman.

Third in the points table was Frank Gardner, who extensively modified his works loaned Lola T190-Chevrolet at the end of the year and scored wins at Thruxton and Silverstone. The Australian in fact narrowly conquered the official works Lola driver, Mike Hailwood, who had a troublesome year in the Epstein/Cuthbert Lola T190-Chevrolet.

For 1971 McLaren, Lola and Surtees brought out new models. McLaren's M18, designed by Gordon Coppuck, using many ideas suggested by the late Bruce McLaren before his tragic accident, was a brand new design that incorporated several Formula 1 ideas. Similarly, the Surtees TS8 was a development of the TS7 Formula 1 car of 1970. Lola's T192 was a long wheelbase version of the 1970 T190 using many innovations developed by their new test driver, Frank Gardner. Lotus updated their 70, while Len Terry designed a brand new Leda known as the LT25.

Thin grids and a lack of competitiveness among the slower entries were still troubles prevalent in early 1971, as in 1970. With such immensely powerful and large cars the wheel to wheel type of racing found in Formula 2 and Formula 3 is not evident in Formula 5000. However, some race promoters say that the public get as much enjoyment watching the really experienced drivers wrestling with their snarling 5-litre machines, as they do seeing a horde of smaller capacity machines constantly changing places. It all goes to provide variety in modern day motor racing. If you like watching big cars that accelerate with a harsh, nearly deafening roar of power, then F5000 is for you. □

Toine Hezemans in the DART/Castrol Chevron B19 heads Guy Edwards in a Lola and Ed Swart in another B19 during a Silverstone race for the cut and thrust 2-litre sports cars.

CHAPTER 6

International sports car racing

'Big bangers' to tiddlers, they all compete
by Mike Cotton

IT IS very difficult, when you think about it, to define a sports car at all these days. It used to be easy when they had two seats, cycle-type mudguards and a couple of spare wheels strapped behind the petrol tank, but nowadays most car makers offer such a range of coupés, fastbacks, twin-cams and twin-carburetter saloons that the original concept is fast disappearing: even 'proper' sports cars like the Lotus Elan have electric winding windows, heaters, and as much comfort as you'd hope to find in an expensive saloon.

In Britain and America plenty of races are organised for sports cars, generally called 'Prodsports' or 'Modsports' to denote the origins of modified production models. Jaguar E-types, TVRs, Lotus Elans, Austin-Healey Sprites and MG Midgets are all extremely popular. The rules state that the car's profile must be nearly original, though a great many modifications are done to the successful models such as fitting wide racing wheels and tyres, five speed gearboxes in some cases, oversize engines, heavy duty brakes, suspension and so on.

These cars fall into a recognised FIA category called Group 4 (Special Grand Touring Cars), and the basic requirement is that at least 500 must have been made.

The Porsche 917's last victory at Le Mans was scored by Dr Helmut Marko/Gijs van Lennep in this Martini Racing Team car.

From the earliest days of motor racing, at the turn of the century until 40 years ago, sports cars were the premier formula and they made up the field for the Grands Prix. In the early thirties the rule about carrying a passenger was abolished, but drivers were still offset to the right, and it was a couple of years before the true single seaters took over. From then on Grand Prix and sports cars went separate ways, the single-seaters to Monaco, Reims, the Nurburgring, Montlhéry and Tunis, while the two-seaters concentrated on longer and more punishing events like Sicily's Targa Florio, the Le Mans 24-Hours and Ireland's Tourist Trophy. Today sports cars still run on closed public roads on the continent, so if the chance to attend the Targa Florio or the Spa 1000 kms should present itself, don't hesitate to go, for they provide wonderful contrasts of fast driving (at the Belgian circuit) and mountain skills.

Until 20 years ago, when car manufacturers were again planning new ranges of models after the war, all the important sports car races featured models like the Jaguar XK120, the Allard J2, Talbots, Healeys, Aston Martin DBs and so on, all cars which were driven to the circuits, raced and driven home again. In fact the final links between road cars and sports cars were probably the Jaguar C- and D-types which were victorious at Le Mans five times in the 1950s. Lofty England and his colleagues at Coventry always drove the cars to Le Mans, often as not Jaguar drivers won, then the cars were driven back! These beautiful machines were the direct predecessors of the Jaguar E-type which was built for sale to the public and announced in 1962.

A phenomenon which appeared first in the early sixties was the mid-engined sports car: Eric Broadley started the trend in 1963 with his Lola GT, a most advanced two-seater with a V8 Ford engine mounted behind

CASTROL GUIDE TO MOTORING SPORT

Interserie racing brings a breath of Can-Am to Europe: here Peter Gethin gets on with the job in the Taylor/Castrol McLaren-Chevrolet.

the seats but ahead of the rear wheels. He had studied the current successful trend in single-seaters, and decided that only a car built on these lines would be correct, in engineering terms, for the task.

Well, the Lola wasn't an outstanding success (it was completed only a couple of days before Le Mans and driven in haste to the Sarthe circuit), but it lasted more than 12 hours and interested a lot of important people. Ford, in Britain and America, asked Eric Broadley to join John Wyer's advanced projects team at Slough, and two years later the Ford GT40—one of motor racing's classic sports cars—was born.

The trend was one of the most significant in the history of motor racing, for it divorced sports cars from road cars, perhaps for ever. A number of production manufacturers have tried, successfully, to make sports cars with mid engines: Colin Chapman's Lotus Europa, the Lamborghini Miura, the Matra M530 and the Volkswagen-Porsche 914 are good examples. Yet so far production has remained extremely low in relation to the market, for in return for outstanding roadholding the customer has to forgo space for himself and his baggage, and perhaps put up with quite a lot of noise too.

This divorce has caused the FIA many problems, for the authorities of motor racing badly wanted to retain the traditional sports car races and in some way convince the public that the cars at Le Mans, or Britain's BOAC 1000 kms, bore some resemblance to the cars in production.

Rules were drawn up for new classes, nowadays called Groups 5, 6 and 7, which catered solely for sports racing cars. The common requirement was for cars to have two seats and bodywork which enclosed the wheels, but beyond that the maker has quite a free hand in his design.

In 1972 Group 5 will be abolished altogether, so we will just briefly mention what it *was* then forget it. The Group 5 rules allowed manufacturers to build cars of their choice *but* 25 identical examples had to be made, and their engine capacity could not be more than 5-litres. They had to have headlights, tail-lights, deep windscreens and carry a spare wheel, all these requirements making the cars suitable for *road use*.

The Ford GT40 conformed ideally. Then a couple of years ago, first Porsche, then Ferrari, built outright two-seater racing cars which just about met the requirements. These two makes established a memorable era in the history of sports car racing, and will perhaps be remembered as the pre-war Mercedes and Auto-Union Grand Prix cars are now. Their 5-litre, fuel injected engines developed 600 horsepower and the highest speeds achieved in a straight line exceeded 230 mph at Spa and Le Mans. A Porsche 917 driven by Jo Siffert established a world record in 1971 for the fastest-ever lap of a road circuit, completing one lap of Belgium's Spa road circuit at an average speed of over 162 mph.

Regrettably, the FIA soon decided that such cars didn't conform with the spirit of sports car rules, and decided to end the sham by abolishing the current Group 5 with a stroke of the pen. In 1972, the World Championship of Makes will be contested only by Group 6 cars (which will be called Group 5!) in just the same guise as before. The present Group 6 means that only one car of a type need be made, but the engine capacity must be not greater than 3-litres. The car must have two seats and enclosed wheel arches, but need not have a spare wheel, lights, luggage space, or even a windscreen.

The Group opens up all sorts of possibilities for motive power, because 3-litre Grand Prix engines are manufactured by Ford-Cosworth, Ferrari, Alfa Romeo and Matra. Other 3-litre racing engines have been made and may be used, including the Martin, the Serenissima, the Porsche 908, even a Renault V8 which didn't work very well in an Alpine a couple of years ago.

Of these, Ferrari spent the 1971 season developing a 3-litre prototype, the 312P, which looked a competitive car for the Championship but strong opposition came from Alfa Romeo, Porsche, Matra and Ford: in fact it was Germany's Porsche firm which took the honours.

A popular new Championship started in 1970 catering for 2-litre prototypes, also running to Group 6 rules (don't forget, Group 5 in 1972). It is called the European 2-litre Championship and the most commonly entered makes come from Britain, made by Eric Broadley's Lola company (the T212) and Derek Bennett's Chevron company (the B19). From Italy, Carlo Abarth has been contesting the Championship seriously with his prototypes using modified Fiat engines, while Lola and Chevron drivers rely on Ford-Cosworth FVC (1.8-litre engines). The racing here is very close and exciting, as you would expect with such similar engines and power outputs.

Another category called Group 7 admits engines of any capacity, but the cars are usually out-and-out powerful monsters. A tentative start was made in Group 7 racing in Britain five or six years ago, but the organisers found that the class was rather an expensive one to offer spectators. Its home then moved to Canada and America when the Sports Car Club of America devised the Can-Am Series. Each year's championship consists of 10 or 11 rounds, all with an enormous amount of prize money, and European teams took the show over with conspicuous success.

Formidable combination: Jacky Ickx in the 3-litre Ferrari 312P.

Rolf Stommelen gets a move on in the 3-litre Alfa Romeo T33.

The cars are almost invariably powered by stock-block Chevrolet engines of 7- or even 8-litres capacity, producing upwards of 700 horsepower. They are light, and the sophisticated racing chassis from the McLaren and Lola works provide the drivers with excellent handling and braking to match the power. The series has become a preserve of the McLaren team in recent years, but Lola has always been a strong challenger along with Jim Hall's Chaparral project, the Castrol-backed BRM, big Ferraris, Porsches, and March, another recently introduced British make.

Group 7 is not exclusively an American formula, because in 1971 a new European series called Interserie was instituted. Nine races were held during the year, bringing to several countries (unfortunately not Britain however) the sight and sound of the world's most powerful cars.

Officially all these Groups come under the heading of sports cars, but the link with true production sports cars is becoming more tenuous all the time. They are, in fact, two seater racing cars the likes of which will never go into serious production for the public. This is not to say that they do not serve a proper purpose, because all the components (which do come from production origins) are being tested severely: fuels, brakes and fluids, oils, clutches, tyres and steering systems. Aerodynamic studies are also being carried out all the time, and undoubtedly the lessons learned do help production car manufacturers like Jaguar, Ferrari, Maserati, Lotus, Porsche and Aston Martin.

Turbine sports cars have been rare, but they too make an interesting study. Rover co-operated with BRM in producing a turbine sports car which ran at Le Mans in 1963 and 1964, winning special prizes. The American Howmet organisation also produced a turbine car later on which contested several rounds of the World Championship for Makes. As yet they lack the sheer power and throttle response of conventional piston engines, but if and when a suitable turbine appears it will probably be tested first in motor racing. Similarly, the Wankel rotary engine appears to offer a good formula for racing, being compact and light. So far it has not been made with sufficient power, but that will probably come in the years ahead, and could revolutionise the shape of motor racing. The German NSU company, holder of the original patent, has experimented with the Wankel in small production sports cars, mainly in local minor hill-climbs, but now that NSU has merged with the huge Volkswagen company the Wankel may benefit from further investment and development.

The most important changes in the next decade will surely be seen in aerodynamics, about which car designers still have much to learn. Aeroplanes of similar size and weight will fly at speeds as low as 70 mph, yet the first objective in racing is to secure stability at speeds up to 250 mph. Stability means predictable handling in a straight line, and through fast and slow corners, and all the effort so far has been channelled into making sports cars stay on the ground! Undulating surfaces, an inherent part of road racing, cause complicating factors, and probably in future more and more fast cars will be developed in wind tunnels with variable factors introduced. The resultant shape may well be a pure wedge, but this guess is only as good as the next man's.

Even if today's sports cars do not look much like your roadgoing model, just remember how much race development has contributed to the design: this contribution will become more and more important as road cars become faster. □

CHAPTER 7

International scene

Around the world on racing wheels!
by Andrew Marriott

MOTOR RACING is very much an international sport and there are few civilised countries in the world without a racing circuit. France can claim to have 'invented' motor racing, but then it quickly spread all over Europe, thence to the United States and now much further afield. Naturally countries with a large motor industry tend to be the strongholds of the sport, like France, the USA, Italy and Britain, which country is nowadays the motor racing 'capital' when it comes to racing car construction. However it is strange to note that, while racing is particularly popular in Sweden, there is not a single permanent racing circuit in the neighbouring country of Norway. In South America there is fantastic enthusiasm for the sport and the average man in Buenos Aires or Rio de Janeiro would probably be able to tell you far more of Jackie Stewart's career than will someone in London or Birmingham.

Nevertheless there is more racing per person in Britain than in any other country in the world and the various chapters in this book give you an insight into everything from our club sport upwards. In this chapter let's take a look at how racing differs around the world.

Watched by an enormous crowd in the stands, the Can-Am racers led by Dan Gurney, followed by Chuck Parsons and Jack Oliver, make an impressive sight at Riverside.

Circuit racing has really caught on in a big way across the Atlantic since the last war, in fact it is now officially said to be the second largest spectator sport in the USA. It is certainly rather more complicated than British racing and offers tremendous variety. In America, circuit racing is split into two distinct categories—road racing and track racing. The road racing is European-style and the track events, held on simple oval circuits, some of them banked like Indianapolis, is unique to North America.

While track racing has been popular in the USA for many years, it is the European-style road racing that has shown enormous growth. The best known road racing championship is the extensively sponsored Can-Am Series which has been dominated by the British McLaren team and their 7- or 8-litre sports racing cars for five years now. Then there is the Continental Championship for Formula A cars which is, of course, where the idea for the British Formula 5000s came from. Yet another very important series of races is called the Trans-Am and these are contested by various works teams running saloon cars. The sight of a field full of Chevrolet Camaros, Ford Boss Mustangs, Javelins and so on driven by America's top drivers is quite something, these events lasting as long as a Grand Prix.

These series are of a national nature and the participants travel all over the States to take part. Naturally, with the great distances involved, American club racing tends to be much more localised. Cars are classified more according to their known performance rather than to actual capacity. Thus the categories start with 'H Production' for the slowest

Above: South African rivals John Love, in the leading Surtees TS9, and Dave Charlton's Lotus 49C keep the crowds happy with their normal brand of hard racing.
Left: Jackie Stewart's appearance in the 1971 Can-Am series, driving the compact 8.1-litre Lola-Chevrolet, gave spectators something to watch apart from race winning McLarens!

sports cars. It sounds rather complicated, but works well in practice: once a year a committee sits to decide if any make of car should be re-graded. If, for instance, the new Triumph Stag proved to be by far the fastest car in a particular class then at the end of that year it would be moved up a category.

Throughout the year championships are run in the various regions and then, in November, the champions and runners-up from each of the eight regions come together at the Road Race of Champions, a series of races from which a National Champion is found in each of the 25 or so categories running, from 'H Prod' with little Sprites, right through to Formula A. All this is organised by the Sports Car Club of America.

In the Southern States still one of the most popular forms of what they call 'Auto Racing' is Stock Cars, run by an organisation called NASCAR. These are not stock cars as we know them in Britain, the bump and bash brigade from Wimbledon and Aldershot stadiums, but enormously fast and powerful production saloons which usually race round banked oval circuits, or Speedways, as they are known. Often the races are something like 350 or 500 miles long and call for several fuel and tyre stops. The cars are completely stripped out, powered by 500+ bhp 7-litre engines and fitted with huge interior roll cages. It is a common sight to see as many as ten of these huge American saloons slipstreaming, or 'drafting' as they call it, round the banked circuits at something over 180 mph. In fact recently, on one of the new steeply banked super-speedways, one of these monster cars recorded a lap speed of over 200 mph! There is a NASCAR Championship race virtually every weekend and the top drivers like Richard Petty, Bobby Isaac and Lee Roy Yarbrough can earn more money than Grand Prix stars.

Also held on banked tracks are the events for the USAC Championship, of which the Indianapolis 500 is by far the most famous of the qualifying rounds. The Indy or USAC cars went through a revolution after 1961, the year that Jack Brabham arrived with an adapted Cooper Grand Prix car. Although he only finished in ninth position, in the decade since then the somewhat old fashioned front engined roadsters, which had for so long dominated the 'Brickyard', have disappeared altogether. Now USAC machines are all rear-engined and look something similar to European Formula 1 cars but are larger and more colourfully painted. The most popular power unit is the 4-cylinder 2.6-litre Offenhauser engine which was originally designed before the war. These engines are turbocharged, which means that the fuel is force-fed into the engine by the aid of the exhaust, and they run on highly potent dope fuel, unlike Grand Prix cars which use normal 5 star pump petrol. These 'Offy' engines, as they are familiarly known, produce a fantastic 700 bhp and driving the cars round the banked oval tracks needs a very special technique. Of all the track racers A. J. Foyt has probably been the most successful, followed closely by Mario Andretti, while brothers Bobby and Al Unser are two of the fastest drivers. Mastering the art of driving on these speedway tracks is difficult, but both Jim Clark and Graham Hill beat the American drivers to win the Indy '500', while Denny Hulme is also now one of the most respected drivers at Indianapolis. Likewise many of the Indy drivers

have been able to adjust to road racing and Andretti has recently become very successful in World Championship events.

Although Indianapolis is by far the best known race on the USAC Championship trail, there are important events every other weekend, some on the super new tracks like Ontario in California, and others on little 1-mile ovals in the smaller towns, which nevertheless bring in huge crowds.

With the vast resources in America, some fantastic motor racing facilities have been built over the past few years. Probably the most spectacular of all is the Ontario Motor Speedway near Los Angeles which cost 23 million dollars to build in 1970. It features a 2½ mile banked oval with a complex of road racing circuits using the main straight and then weaving about in the infield. There is also a drag strip, while the facilities for mechanics, press and so on set new standards. Grandstand seating for 140,000 people is provided where they can watch their racing in comfort.

Back in Europe motor racing closely follows the pattern in Britain although a few of the genuine road circuits, where streets are closed to traffic so that the race can take place, still exist. Regrettably, the authorities are making such races increasingly difficult to hold. Some of these road races (like Monaco and Pau) are on short town circuits while others like Spa in Belgium, Brno in Czechoslovakia, and the gran'daddy of them all, the Targa Florio in Sicily, sweep for miles through the countryside.

Another European speciality is the mountain climbs which can be very spectacular and have their own FIA approved Championship. These are races up the sides of mountains against the clock and, unlike the British hill climbs which often last little more than 30 seconds a run, the European climbs wind up the hillsides for possibly five miles or more. Mountain climbs are particularly popular in Switzerland where circuit racing has been banned by the government since the 1955 Le Mans disaster.

Some excellent and very competitive motor racing goes on in countries such as Australia, New Zealand, South Africa and Canada. The latter close neighbour of the USA is very much a part of international motor sport with several promising drivers based there, a round of the

Saloon car racing is popular in America (left), and in New Zealand where this sliding V8 Falcon (above) was photographed.

World Championship every year and some testing circuits such as St Jovite. Apart from circuit racing, Canadians also share the Scandinavian love of ice racing—a truly spectacular sport where cars jostle for positions at over 80 mph in long power slides!

South Africa shares with Canada the distinction of holding a Grand Prix every year and the country also acts as host to a series of International grade races for sports cars—the Springbok events. The best known track in the country is Kyalami, near Johannesburg, a circuit which is usually chosen for the annual Formula 1 Championship event. South Africa has three or four really top class drivers who keep in practice with former works Formula 1 machinery or F5000-style machines in the country's own annual championship. Men such as John Love, Dave Charlton and Jackie Pretorius can hold their heads up in the best company, whilst Willie Ferguson and young Jody Scheckter should further enhance the country's reputation in the future.

Australia and New Zealand share the Tasman winter single seater Championship between them—a series which, in the past, attracted the best European Formula 1 drivers to bring 2.5-litre versions of their normal mounts to meet the challenge of these fertile breeding grounds for world class drivers. Remember that New Zealand has produced such notable drivers as Bruce McLaren, Chris Amon and Denis Hulme, while Jack Brabham originally came to Britain from Australia. Both 'down under' countries also provide many of the best racing mechanics to be found today, while future Australian World Champion hope Tim Schenken shares something of Brabham's mechanical abilities.

In common with South Africa, Australia has an exceptionally varied selection of racing saloons — anything that will physically hold an American-inspired V8 will do so!

Motor racing is also thriving behind the Iron Curtain although details are rather hard to come by! Czechoslovakia, Yugoslavia and

Left: The world's richest race is the annual Indianapolis 500; this McLaren, driven by Peter Revson, averaged nearly 180 mph during a qualifying lap!

Above: Group 2 saloon cars at the start of a Czechoslovakian race.

Right: Ontario Motor Speedway in California offers every amenity to the spectator, save that of getting too close to the action!

East Germany are countries the western competitors visit quite regularly for Formula 3 races. These countries also build their own single seater machines although they are somewhat crude by our standards. Touring car racing is also very popular behind the Iron Curtain, with several events for the European Touring Car Championship being held in the countries mentioned. So far Western competitors have not ventured into Russia, but that country's space age designers could shake up the established order of things if ever the USSR decides motor racing is nationally prestigious!

As we said earlier, racing is very popular in South America, particularly in Brazil and Argentina where some very skilled drivers have been produced over the last couple of years, reflecting the healthy state of racing in those countries. A rather special aspect of South American motor racing is that, although there are some very good circuits, racing on the open roads from town to town is very popular, particularly through the mountain ranges and spectacular countryside in places like Peru and Chile.

In the Far East, particularly in countries where British servicemen have been based, racing round often highly dangerous street circuits is very popular. Countries like Macau and Singapore have their own Grand Prix events for a mixture of single seater cars. In Japan racing is steadily growing in popularity and there is an excellent circuit at Fuji but as yet this successful industrial country, which now produces so many automobiles, has yet to produce any really notable drivers. When they do no doubt there will be a Japanese GP in the World Championship series.

So you can see that motor racing is far from being a sport enjoyed by only Europe and North America. Almost every week comes news of a race in another far-off land as motoring sport continues to spread all over the world. □

CHAPTER 8

British club racing

The colourful world of amateurs
by Mike Doodson

NOT EVERYONE can be World Champion, but there are 22,000 people who must at least dream about it, for that is the number of competition licences issued in 1970 by the Royal Automobile Club. Of course, many of those licences were issued to rally drivers, others to hillclimb competitors and still more to the agricultural Fangios who get so much fun out of autocrossing in their own club events.

On a rather more intense scale, club racing is the weekend sport for a surprisingly large number of people, sometimes 200 of them at a well supported race meeting. And there can be as many as ten club level meetings on a busy Bank Holiday weekend in Britain, so even if your mathematics are bad, you'll have realised that club racing is indeed popular.

At its higher levels, club racing has all the intensity and competitiveness of a Grand Prix. An important meeting at Silverstone or Brands Hatch, with points at stake in some notable national championship, will attract the champions of the future. And the quality of our racing is recognised throughout the world, as you can prove for yourself if

Mini Seven Club racing is a cheap and cheerful way of competing.

CASTROL GUIDE TO MOTORING SPORT

you listen to the dozen or so different languages and accents which can be heard in almost any British club racing paddock all year round.

Why is Britain the most active club racing country of the world? We have the obvious advantages of geographical compactness and plenty of circuits, but that isn't the whole story. Britons tend to develop manias about their hobbies, from butterfly collecting to fox hunting, and our passion for motor racing dates back to the dear dead days of Brooklands before the war. In the past quarter century there's been less of the 'right crowd and no crowding' tradition in racing and it's all become very democratic. It may not please the diehards but it fills the circuits with spectators.

This pool of top line club pilots produced the first British aces for the teams which started to spring up in Formula 1 after the war. When British teams actually started winning Grand Prix events, it was almost as though Britain's cars and drivers were swamping the field. Since then, this country has taken over from Italy the mantle of being the centre of European racing, and the home of most major manufacturers. Those new British drivers had all been raised in the hurly-burly of club racing or hillclimbing: who could forget Stirling Moss hillclimbing his motor-cycle-engined Cooper, or Mike Hawthorn hurling his pre-war Riley around Goodwood?

To get an inside opinion on the present state of club racing, I spoke to Barry Bland, Competitions Secretary, British Automobile Racing Club. The BARC has a larger racing membership than any other of the race organising British clubs, with regional centres which also run their own meetings. Most of the spadework has to be done from London, however, and the responsibility for this lies in Barry's hands.

Organising a race meeting is a tremendous task and the work starts well over 12 months in advance. Permits must be obtained from the Royal Automobile Club (which sanctions every race meeting in the country, wherever it takes place), the circuit must be booked and regulations have to be sent out with at least three months to go.

But that's only the start of the job and the pace quickens as the entry forms roll in. Barry has as many as eight meetings 'on the boil' at any one time. 'There are hundreds of details to be attended to,' he says. 'Quite apart from the entries, we have ambulances and fire engines to be arranged, hospitals to be notified, timekeepers, doctors, scrutineers and many other people with specialised qualifications to be appointed. We must have adequate officials, and even a club meeting at Thruxton could require as many as 240 marshals, most of whom are keen enthusiasts from among the club's membership.'

The BARC runs its own championships and although this is not Barry's job there is the problem of finding a sponsor for the bigger meetings and the club's championships. More often than not, race day is exciting and enjoyable, but it can be spoiled if the weather turns out to be wet, keeping away the crowds upon whom the organisers rely, or if competitors who have sent in entry forms (and fees) fail to arrive. This is a problem which nobody can predict until it is too late and I asked Barry what he felt. 'Yes, the high number of non-starters is depressing,' he agreed, 'but it seems to be common to everyone. It is very difficult to control and the only consolation for us is that we still have their entry fees to help offset the expense of organisation.'

A typical club meeting, whether it is organised by the BARC or any of the other major clubs, is a noisy, colourful affair. There are usually half a dozen races, seldom of more than 10 or 15 laps, one of which may be the day's 'feature' event. Practice starts early in the morning and afterwards each competitor pulls the other's leg about how much faster he's going to go in the race. But there's a serious side, too, and the officials can't relax their concentration at any time. Motor racing, after all, is dangerous and the message gets across when you see the number of doctors present listed in the programme.

Happily, the non-injurious incidents far outnumber the ones which involve hospitalisation. But the question is often asked why normally sober citizens should spend small fortunes in search of prizes which represent only a fraction of what they have spent on buying their car and keeping it at the top of its form. Their answers would all be that they consider racing to be a modern, exciting sport, though you would be well advised not to ask anyone whose bent motor car is being trailed in after hitting a barrier, or while he contemplates a big hole in the side of his engine where a connecting rod has just found a way out!

Where should you start if you want to go racing? Much depends, of course, on your mechanical aptitude and the amount of money you are prepared to spend. Sit down and work out a budget: then double it, because there's bound to be something you have overlooked! Don't be too disheartened, because there are many people who go racing on less money than their workmates would spend on a foreign holiday or a new car.

One of the best ways to start is to buy an old Mini and turn it into a racing saloon. There's a well supported class for 850 Minis and championship events, organised by the Mini Seven Club, are invariably very cut-throat affairs fought out by machines which can be built by an enthusiast for around £250. In complete contrast, you may find yourself parked in the paddock alongside someone who's bought one of last year's Formula 1 cars and is whizzing round in an ultimate attempt to beat the Formula Fords. And if you have to ask how much a year-old Grand Prix car costs, then you certainly can't afford one!

Between that Mini and the Formula 1 machine you'll find a bewildering variety of classes for every imaginable type of car. Saloons come in as many as four classes in one race alone, and as long as its silhouette bears a likeness to the same car in the dealer's showroom, then it's acceptable. That lets in such alarming creations as a Ford Capri using a Ford V8 and suspension from a Lola-Chevrolet sports car, which at least made a change from its owner's previous hobby of cramming Jaguar engines into Ford Anglias. Hybrid saloons are fairly common these days, but for sheer ingenuity I can't recall anything to beat a couple of Minis put together by Harry Ratcliffe a few years back. The first had a $3\frac{1}{2}$-litre Buick V8 engine mounted in the boot, driving the front wheels via a Jaguar differential. Ashen faced after his one and only race with that, Harry consigned the Mini-Buick to street use only (!) and put his mind to constructing one with a normal engine mounted in the boot and driving the rear wheels. It was just on the point of being sorted out when it perished in a fire: nobody has tried the idea again.

54

Above: John Wales in smooth form, driving a Volkswagen powered Royale SuperVee at Thruxton.

Left: F1200 and 750F cars provide cheap sport for ingenious constructors.

Below: Variety is the spice of club saloon car dicing; here the leading Viva is being driven by an unusually restrained Gerry Marshall, pursued by Thruxton Mini ace Richard Longman.

Above: The 1.6-litre Clubmans cars travel very quickly, none more so than Ray Mallock's U2 which leads this entertaining bunch.
Left: That Capri is partially glass fibre and is propelled by a 5-litre V8 engine, all put together by driver Mike Hill, who is shown fending off the desperate advances of Alec Poole's turbocharged Mini.

Sports cars have always been popular, of course, though this class seems to be on the wane at present. Nevertheless, a mixed bag of AC Cobras and Chevron GTs can make an entertaining race. One class unique to Britain is the Clubman's Formula, originally for 'Lotus Seven type' cars. The Lotus Sevens don't get much of a look-in these days, largely because there has been a great upsurge of interest in the class, which is even served by its own Register and has a popular championship. Many of us feel that a championship clubman's formula race represents the odd-ball British amateur racing at its best, giving the lie to the old American saying that if you give an Englishman a sheet of metal, he's bound to do something silly with it.

So don't run away with the idea that because these Clubman's devices look a bit crude they are unscientific. Far from it, their designers often choose the class simply because there's so much room for experiment and the cost of something which doesn't work can be measured in terms of a few feet of alloy sheet, some cold-drawn tubing and the inevitable sleepless nights.

Everyone has to start somewhere and there are several top designers who trace their beginnings in racing back to these little sports cars with flapping cycle type wings and a token passenger seat. Some 20 years ago, one of the most promising young club racing drivers was busy developing his own 750 Special, powered by a tuned pre-war Austin Seven engine, in a North London lock-up garage. His name was Colin Chapman and he called the car a Lotus, the first of a line which went on to win four Formula 1 Constructors' Championships.

The first Lola was an 1172 Special (powered by a side valve Ford engine), the designer of which, Eric Broadley, is now the boss of a company which has won Indianapolis and exports millions of dollars worth of cars to the United States.

Both Broadley and Chapman were originally members of the 750 Motor Club, which continues to be associated with the same type of 'poor man's racing' today. The side valve Austin and Ford engines have been superseded by more modern ohv equivalents and these days the tyres are a little wider and smaller in diameter, but the racing is as good as ever and it is just as likely that there's a future F1 constructor among them. Arthur Mallock, who started racing 750s at the same time as Chapman, is still making front engined cars with non-independent rear suspension. He only does it as a part time business and now that he has given up driving, his two sons have taken over. Between them they hold lap records all over the country in two classes, Clubman's and Formula Ford.

It is in the field of single seaters that club racing has changed most over the past five years. Not so long ago, a single seater racing car was rare at any race meeting. Nowadays the single seaters are liable to outnumber the other entries, and most of them are Formula Fords. The principle of putting a standard 1500 cc pushrod engine into a Formula 3 chassis first occurred to the owner of a racing school with a big stack of invoices in his hand, all for repairing the expensive high revving F3 units which had been ruined by the over eager and ham-fisted would-be champions among his pupils. Nowadays, 1600 cc engines are allowed, along with limited tuning. John Webb, who is the managing director of Motor Circuit Developments (the company which controls five of Britain's motor racing circuits), immediately recognised the potential of this class and arranged for public races to be organised. The success of the formula has now outstripped even Mr Webb's wildest dreams and there are probably more than 300 Formula Fords in Britain and an even greater number in Europe, South Africa, America and Australia, throughout which countries the Formula has been very well received.

Why does a driver go overboard for a single seater when he would probably stand a much better chance of winning in a sports or saloon car? The answer, I believe, is that anyone who is even vaguely interested in racing is a frustrated Grand Prix star at heart and the nearest he can get to a Formula 1 car is in a Formula Ford at a cost of between £1000 and £1500. And if you look at the lap speed records, you'll find that Formula Fords are now going round Silverstone faster than Fangio did in his 1957 Formula 1 Maserati!

This enthusiasm for single seaters appears to be spreading and the latest spectator surveys show that the paying public now enjoys Formula Ford and Formula 3, even in preference to some of the longer established saloon and sports car classes.

With so many cars and drivers, club racing could almost be said to be getting out of hand. Some circuit owners even run races all year round, yet the last people to complain are the drivers. It's all a part of the enthusiasm for racing which has made Britain the world's number one racing power. Join in yourself: if you can't afford a car, become a club member and learn to marshal. Who knows, before long they might even issue you with one of those luminous Castrol jackets! ☐

CHAPTER 9/part 1

A classic event

The story of riding alongside Stirling Moss
by Denis Jenkinson

IT NEVER ceases to amaze me that even after more than 15 years people
still recall the occasion in 1955 when Stirling Moss won the Mille Miglia
race at a record average speed of 97.8 mph, driving the 1000 mile course
round Italy without respite for 10hrs 07mins 48secs, only stopping for
28 seconds at Pescara for petrol and 60 seconds at Rome for new rear tyres
and petrol. Somehow this exploit of Great Britain's most well-known
racing driver caught the imagination of everyone, not only in his own
country but all over the world. Admittedly it was a remarkable feat of
endurance and skill, but probably the reason it is remembered even now,
where many of his great racing exploits are long forgotten, is that at the
time he took a first-class Public Relations man with him on that trip.
After the race this fellow wrote up the whole day's racing, and more
besides, in a manner never done before or since, for the simple reason that
the situation had not occurred before, nor has it occurred since, and is
unlikely ever to happen again. This story was printed at great length in
Motor Sport for June 1955 under the initials DSJ, the pen-name of the
writer of this article. Drivers had won the Mille Miglia before and thousands of other races, but never before had every detail of the race been

Left: Stirling Moss does the talking whilst author Denis Jenkinson secures his crash helmet.
Above: The Mercedes-Benz 300 SLR sets off on its successful 1000 mile journey, urged onward by the wildly enthusiastic Italian crowd.

committed to paper; usually a driver's greatest race received only a word picture as seen from the Press stand, or at best from some interesting part of the circuit. By sheer chance, coupled with a passionate enthusiasm for the Mille Miglia, I was able to sit in the passenger seat of the Mercedes-Benz 300 SLR that Moss drove, on the understanding that, win or lose, I was there for my own enjoyment and his benefit. I told the Editor and Proprietor of *Motor Sport*, for whom I was, and still am, Continental Correspondent, that in their June issue they would either get the story of a lifetime or I would get an obituary notice. I'm glad to say they got the former. Since that story appeared exclusively in the monthly 'green 'un' it has been bought, borrowed, stolen, copied, plagiarised, abbreviated, enlarged, butchered and mentioned in just about every country where motor racing has a following, and consequently the 1955 Mille Miglia became Stirling Moss's greatest exploit in most peoples' minds. As I say, he unwittingly took a good PR man with him.

The real reason I went along was nothing to do with journalism at all, a passenger or co-driver was required by the regulations, dating back to the beginning of the Mille Miglia in 1927, for then no-one visualised being able to drive the whole race on his own. In actual fact 1955 was the first year that a passenger or co-driver was optional. From its inception the length of the race was 1000 miles, usually forming a figure of eight up and down Italy, from Brescia in the north to Rome in the south, with the crossing point at Bologna, the total distance being in the order of 1600 kilometres, which is 1000 old Roman miles, hence the name Mille Miglia. Motor racing was begun by the French before the end of the 19th Century with town-to-town races, such as Paris–Bordeaux, Paris–Vienna, Paris–Rouen and so on, and when circuit racing took over in 1903 the town-to-town events died. The Italians resurrected the idea with the Mille Miglia, and the pity of it was that it was the Automobile Club of Brescia who did so, for throughout the life of the race the newspaper and political factions in Milan, who were democratically inclined, fought a constant battle against the factions in Brescia who were socialist inclined. This political wrangling went on between Milan and Brescia over every possible activity, and each year at Mille Miglia time the race was used for more slanging matches, especially if there was any trouble in the event. When the Marquis de Portago, and his passenger Eddy Nelson, crashed in 1957 and were killed, along with 11 spectators, only a few miles from the finish at Brescia, the newspapers made the most of the occasion, for the reporters could actually get to the scene of the accident and enlarge their stories beyond all reason. Accidents that happened 500 or 600 miles away got little mention, except in the local papers of San Benedetto del Tronto, or Acquapendente or any other obscure parts of the south. The 1957 accident was too near home for comfort and after much political slanging and haranguing the democrats of Milan won a major political victory over the socialists of Brescia by persuading the Government to ban the Mille Miglia for all time.

I was fortunate in being able to enjoy the last phase of its history, when it reached a climax, and to witness and take part in an era of motor racing that is long since dead but will live forever in history. In 1953 I stood by the roadside and watched Ferraris, Alfa Romeos, Maseratis, Aston Martins and Jaguars pass by within inches of my feet, each one carrying a passenger or co-driver, and I immediately thought 'that's for me'. The following year I went in the passenger's seat of an HWM-Jaguar with George Abecassis but our progress was stopped after 200 miles by a broken shock-absorber. In 1955 I rode with Moss in the victorious Mercedes-Benz 300 SLR and in 1956 I went with him in a special 3½ litre Maserati and we went over the side of a mountain in the pouring rain just before halfway. In the last race to be run I was again with Moss in a 4½ litre V8 Maserati and it broke just 7 miles from the start.

Many people had the impression that the Mille Miglia was an event all of its own, but this was not so, for throughout the Italian racing calender there were similar events, but none so long or so vast in its organisation. Racing on the normal public roads, closed by the police and the army, was the recognised thing in Italy, on short circuits for Grand Prix cars, or long town-to-town routes for sports cars, and these developed rugged and durable sports cars as well as saloon cars, for there were classes for everything. There was a whole season of long sports car races in most of the provinces, the route usually being around the mountains for 200 or 300 miles and they took the title of The Giro (or Tour) of such and such, like the Giro di Umbria, the Giro di Calabria, the Giro di Toscana and the Giro di Sicilia and a lot of people thought that these were some sort of rally. In a way they were, for competitors started at intervals of 30 seconds or 1 minute and had a route card that had to be stamped at key points, usually the central square in any major town that the route passed through, but the main difference from rallying was that from start to finish it was a flat out blind, or special stage, the fastest man was the winner, rules and regulations were few and the cars were out-and-out racing cars, even thinly-disguised Grand Prix cars.

The Mille Miglia was the Big One, and to win this was the ambition of every Italian racing driver, as it was of every sports car manufacturer, and after competing in the various Giros, everyone entered for the ultimate

Giro, the Mille Miglia, in which entries were as high as 600. One or two factories would send a works car to some of the smaller events as a try-out before entering a full team of four or six cars in the big one, and I well remember the excitement in Palermo in 1954 when Umberto Maglioli took part in the Giro Sicilia in a works 4.9 litre Ferrari, this being a short 600 mile try out before the full team entered for the 1000 mile race, the really big one.

It was generally accepted in racing circles that it was a hopeless task for a non-Italian car to win the Mille Miglia, as the Italians had the advantage of knowing the country and the roads, and it was impossible for anyone visiting the country for the race to learn a circuit of 1000 miles length. In addition, most of the top Italian drivers had grown up in the series of Giros, probably starting in their local event with a small saloon and graduating to sports cars with an eye on an eventual drive in a factory car. In 1931 a Mercedes-Benz SSK driven by Caracciola had won the Mille Miglia, this being the only occasion a non-Italian car and driver had won the race, until in 1955 Mercedes-Benz entered with four 300 SLR racing/sports cars. They had entered in 1952 with 300 SL coupes, and finished second, but in 1955 they were out to win, with Fangio, Moss, Kling and Herrmann as drivers. In the early years of the race it was quite usual for two top drivers to share a car, though they were seldom happy in the passenger's seat, but the more usual thing was for a driver to take a number one mechanic with him. This was for three reasons, first to mend anything that broke or help with pit stops, second to do some of the easier driving if the driver got tired, and third for company, for many drivers found

---

Even judged by today's standards the Mercedes 300 SLR was a sleek and efficient machine, capable of speeds up to 175 mph.

1000 miles a long and lonely trip on their own, and liked to have someone alongside to shout at occasionally. Many of the factory mechanics were a bit reluctant to ride in the race, but often had to accept it as part of their job, and it was thanks to one such mechanic that I got my first ride in the Mille Miglia. Frank Nagle was the mechanic looking after the HWM-Jaguar in 1954 and when Abecassis entered he told Frank that he would be riding in the passenger seat 'to keep me company, as it's a helluva long way' said George. When I arrived in Brescia about a week before the event and asked if I could go in the HWM, Abecassis said I had better ask Frank. I've never met anyone who said 'Yes, of course' so quickly as Frank. Before the event Abecassis said he had better take me for a quick dash up the local Autostrada so that I could see what the car was like, and as I had never been at more than 110 mph in my life before, Frank gave me a splendid piece of advice. He said 'When you get over 130 mph it makes you put your comic away and sit up and take notice'. He was absolutely right, and I thoroughly enjoyed the 150 mph test run.

Late in 1954 I was watching the new sports/racing Mercedes-Benz on test at Monza along with John Fitch, the American racing driver who was living in Italy at the time. We fell to discussing the Mille Miglia and why the Italians had such an advantage and we formulated a plan whereby a non-Italian driver could win the race with the aid of a human computer in the form of a passenger. That the new Mercedes-Benz sports car was the car to win was agreed unanimously. We reckoned that by long and careful planning it should be possible to put the whole route down on paper and for the passenger to transmit this to the driver as they went along. This appealed to me enormously for I had on two occasions done a basically similar thing when I was racing as a sidecar passenger. Once in 1949 at the Mont Ventoux mountain hill-climb, when my rider was worried by three dodgy corners that he could not remember accurately, I concentrated on land marks for them and thumped his foot appropriately as we approached them. The second time was at the Nurburgring in 1950, with a Belgian sidecar rider who was hopeless at remembering long circuits; there I developed a system of thumps on his foot to denote the severity of a corner, and a tweak of the toe-cap of his boot to right or left to indicate the direction to expect to have to turn. On both occasions the idea had worked splendidly. I had also been intrigued by the knowledge that one of the Porsche drivers in 1954 had taken a passenger with him to read some pace-notes, and various other drivers had used passengers for similar things in the past. Previously the idea had only been applied to general overall principles of terrain and town plans, this time we intended to spend three months at preparation and log every unseen bump and corner and difficult point in the whole 1000 miles. When Stirling Moss was signed up by Mercedes-Benz, John Fitch lost the opportunity to drive a 300 SLR sports car, and had to accept a 300 SL production coupé which could not hope to win, and as Moss approached me with a view to doing some pace-note reading for him, John Fitch sportingly agreed to abandon our project and let me join Moss and take along all our plans for the defeat of the Italians. The plan with Fitch was that I would be in full charge of the car and he would merely steer it under my directions, that we would develop a system that would tell me exactly where we were on the road and I would transmit to him, by some means to be developed, what was about to happen and what he should be doing. Our basic plan was so complex that I visualized lying down out of sight with a group of instruments to study and interpret. When I got down to the business with Moss it became a lot simpler, for his time was limited and anyway he was not prepared to put his faith in me and the idea 100 per cent. The compromise worked well however, and after some 12,000 miles I had everything logged down on an 18 foot roll of paper and we had a system of hand signals by means of which we could communicate. Eventually he had complete confidence in me and the idea and we won the race, more or less faultlessly, saving as much as 30 minutes of time in his estimation.

Some of the time saving that occurred was when braking at the end of a long 170 mph straight. Our system told him the latest point to shut off for what was happening at the end of the straight, saving seconds over some-one who could only go on what he could see and remember. We could take blind brows at 170 mph without easing back on the accelerator, whereas others would probably lift off and drop to 150 mph until they could see the next move. We could take blind corners flat out, knowing that a long straight followed; we knew exactly where the control points were and the latest braking points for them; we could accelerate round blind corners and over hills as fast as the car would go; we could take ess bends and humps at the fastest possible speeds, it was all logged down on my 'toilet roll'. At no time did Moss have to ease back on the accelerator and wonder what was round the next corner, or over the next brow, or if we turned left or right at the end of the main street in Ancona or Siena. A 10 mile circuit can be learnt off by heart, but a 1000 mile circuit is impossible without years of practice. One of the first persons I met after the race was John Fitch, who simply said 'so the idea worked.'

Alas, such events are a thing of the past, the nearest today being short special stages on rallies, with uncontrollable saloon cars, which do not interest me at all. It was the challenge of the 'big one' that fascinated me about the Mille Miglia. Before the 1955 event I had a similar system planned for the Giro di Sicilia, as a try out, but unfortunately it fell through, so it was straight in at the deep end. That 1955 event was only the second time a non-Italian driver had won the race, and the only time a British driver won it, and the record speed must stand for ever, like the record average of 63 mph set up by Gabriel from Paris–Bordeaux in 1903 in the ill fated Paris–Madrid race, when it was abandoned because of bad accidents on the way to Bordeaux. My only regret is that in 1957 our Maserati broke down, for we were both confident that we could have chopped off the 7 mins 48 secs of our 1955 time, and achieved a neat 1000 miles in 10 hours, for that big Maserati would out-accelerate the Mercedes-Benz 300 SLR and had a maximum speed of over 180 mph. After three years of planning we knew just about all there was to know about average speed potential round the Mille Miglia route. Talking with Moss in later years, we often speculated as to how fast a Ford GT40 would have completed the course, or today whether a Porsche 917 could average 120 mph for the whole circuit. The thought of doing 230 mph along the roads where we were flat out at 175 mph in 1955 is most intriguing.

I still meet people who say 'you must have been mad in 1955' or 'you were very brave' but the ones I enjoy talking to are those who merely say 'Lucky devil, I'd have given my right arm to have had the opportunity.' ☐

A 180 mph ride in Can-Am style

by Michael Tee

I KNEW BEFORE I squeezed myself beside Bruce McLaren in his bright orange McLaren Can-Am racing car that this could be the ride of a lifetime. However, not even my most vivid dreams came near to the exhilarating truth of swooping around an American race track, touching over 180 miles an hour alongside the New Zealander who designed and drove the almost invincible Can-Am cars which bore his name. Less than a year after I shared the cramped driver's quarters of this 600 horsepower monster with McLaren, he was dead, tragically killed whilst testing a development of the car in which I had been passenger. Today the name lives on through Bruce McLaren Motor Racing Ltd, based at Colnbrook near London Airport, where single seaters for Formula 1 and Indianapolis are made together with the Can-Am McLarens which have taken three Championships in this richly rewarded series.

The author is wedged alongside Bruce McLaren, whilst chief mechanic Tyler Alexander advises McLaren and Denis Hulme looks worried!

In 1969 the McLaren M8B model won ten out of ten Can-Am races and on occasion proved capable of returning faster lap times than Formula 1 cars. The final round of the Can-Am Championship was at Riverside Raceway in California and it was at that track that I joined McLaren and his team for an open practice session. By the time I arrived at the track, which was basking in customary Californian sunshine, the butterflies in my stomach had turned into a feeling of sick apprehension at what was to come. A preliminary briefing from the Goodyear tyre technicians did not help to soothe my nerves either, for they soon told me how much braking and cornering forces had multiplied since my last ride as a passenger in a racing Aston Martin some ten years previously. The massive disc brakes and terrifically wide, squat, tyres enabled the M8B to slow down and then flash through corners at some $1\frac{1}{2}$ times G force, so I realized that I would literally have to wedge myself in the skimpy space allowed by the regulations for an imaginary passenger—though it would need a 'Gnome of Zurich' to feel at home on such a perch!

After I had wriggled my way inside Bruce's spare overalls and donned an all-enclosing Bell Star helmet, the mechanics set about installing my ample frame alongside McLaren. With one hand behind the driver firmly gripping the roll bar mounted above, the mechanics warned me that things could literally get pretty hot as the oil and water pipes passed alongside my overalls.

My initial impression was of the marvellous view ahead, which was much better than in the Porsche 911 I owned at that time. During the next half hour I had the best view one could possibly have of a top class driver (and probably the world's best development driver) at work in his natural element.

First, we rumbled away to cover two laps at no more than 3000 rpm, before calling at the pits to check the car over, prior to fully extending this, one of the world's fastest two seaters. Even during this warming up period my body felt as though it was a passenger in a particularly rapidly driven road car. As we went under a bridge in top gear Bruce even took his hands off the tiny leather rimmed steering wheel to demonstrate how well the car could cruise along without him!

Although my nerves were now completely calm, it did cross my mind that if what I had just experienced was a Sunday afternoon drive for a McLaren/McLaren combination, what would the real thing be like? Even mentally doubling our speed in every conceivable situation was not enough to give a true idea of the next 25 minutes and 14 laps, by the end of which our two up McLaren had travelled fast enough to qualify for thirteenth place on the race-day grid.

Now that we were using over 6000 rpm, the 1500 lb car was fairly shooting from corner to corner, barely giving me time to brace myself before the next bend inexorably tugged me to and fro. In fact we were travelling so quickly that we began to overtake quite a few of the other cars: I shall long remember the look Chris Amon gave the pair of us as we swept past his Ferrari between turns 6 and 7! Not quite so pleasant was the small bombardment of pebbles and dust bestowed upon us by the driver of another rapid car which we were forced to follow.

With the 7100 cc Chevrolet V8 bellowing furiously behind us, I found that we lined up for turn 1 at some 140 mph in third gear: at that speed the idea of actually racing through the corner seems madness. However, we emerged unscathed the other side and hurtled into a series of ess bends, the driver's foot flashing between hard braking and equally violent acceleration as we entered the complex of four curves, continuing to gain speed swiftly in third gear until we dived into the braking area for the U-shaped turn 6. Here I could really watch McLaren masterfully controlling the car as he quickly changed straight from third to first gear, powering it out on the other side with the rear wheels slipping equally swiftly outwards. A couple of twitches on the pinhead-accurate steering and the orange machine gobbled up the short straight to turn 7, a reverse U curve which also demanded first gear. The power was half on as the McLaren plummetted over the brow of the corner to shoot towards the eighth turn in third gear. Once again Bruce's hand whipped the tiny gearlever through the gate from third to first gear, and again I was shoved firmly away from McLaren as his hands darted round the steering wheel, blending the car into a vicious corner which progressively tightened up.

Mercifully the G-forces ceased bending me to their whims and a long straight appeared ahead as the car was snicked through the gears to zip towards the end as though connected by a taut elastic band. Instead of doing a hands-off 80 mph under that bridge my head was forced back by a 170 mph gale. The tachometer indicated just over 6000 revolutions and we were thundering along at a windy but exhilarating 180 miles an hour, then the car's nose dipped and the brakes hauled us back to the land of sliding second gear reality. Turn 9 is the wide final curve of the course and it was taken with unremitting force in second gear, followed by a snatch change into third and past the grinning McLaren mechanics!

Although I was lightly fried by the cooling and lubrication pipes inside the cockpit, and my gripping hand and arm felt as if they had been welded on to the roll bar, I was pulled out quite convinced that this really was the finest way to see a motor race, though I would not want to sit alongside anyone of lesser driving ability than that which Bruce McLaren displayed to me on that hot morning.

Incidentally our best lap time of 1 m 42 s translated as an *average* speed of 116.5 mph—not bad going when the car had to carry someone who weighed more than an extra full load of fuel! ☐

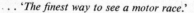
. . . *'The finest way to see a motor race.'*

The aspiring professional driver

by Andrew Marriott

THE LETTERS continue to pour into the racing magazines from hopeful 14 year olds saying that they have decided to become racing drivers when they grow up and please can they have the address of Gold Leaf-Team Lotus! Unfortunately neither GLTL nor the labour exchange have any vacancies for racing drivers at the moment, and are never likely to.

Any racing driver competing in a car which he has not had to pay for out of his own money has got a considerable talent of one kind or another. Perhaps he is an expert at chatting up the advertising agencies and persuading them that one of their clients should sponsor his racing car, or possibly he was fortunate enough to have a rich friend to sponsor him, or maybe he has a genuine talent which marks him out as a man destined for the top. But one thing is certain, by then he has many racing miles behind him already.

Take Colin Vandervell for instance, the 26 year old son of the late Vanwall Grand Prix car constructor, millionaire Tony Vandervell. In 1971 Colin Vandervell was driving a Formula 3 car loaned to him by the Brabham factory and entered under the auspices of Bell & Colvill Racing with Castrol. The smart Brabham is painted in the bright livery of the Castrol oil company, not for philanthropic reasons but because Castrol believe that Colin's efforts on the tracks really will promote the product and help to sell more motor oil.

Well, it is obvious that Colin Vandervell has all the best connections in the racing world with his father's background and so on . . . or is it? In fact, like so many of Britain's promising drivers, including Bev Bond, Roger Williamson and Tony Brise, Colin Vandervell first made his name driving karts, principally because his famous father forbade him to race anything larger, and therefore it wasn't until his father died that he actually took to full scale racing.

It was the summer of 1969 before Colin had saved up enough of his own money to buy a Lotus Formula Ford, just as many hundreds of other drivers have done. But Vandervell junior not only had the natural talent to do well, he also had that strain of ruthlessness. Soon he had changed the Lotus for a secondhand Merlyn and thrown in his lot with an engine tuner called Denis Rowland. From then on Vandervell kept winning in Formula Ford and during the 1970 season he chalked up over 20 victories, took the British Formula Ford Championship, was a narrow second in the European Championship and won the premier £500 Grovewood Award, the top accolade a promising British driver can receive.

Formula 3 is full of tough young drivers who want to make it to the top. This six-car bunch is on Silverstone's last corner—the site of many spectacular moves as the drivers race for the flag. In this picture Colin Vandervell in the Brabham BT 35 is towing Barrie Maskell's square-fronted Chevron, and the successful Lotus works driver from Australia, Dave Walker.

This obviously put Vandervell in a position to do some hard bargaining. He had also shown up well in a few late season Formula 3 races driving a works backed March. Not surprisingly, when the end of the season came there were several offers for him to sort through. Some of them were not sufficiently attractive but in the end he had to decide between two good opportunities. Here we see that becoming a top professional racing driver does not end on the track. Obviously Vandervell had to make a decision, and he chose the Brabham with backing from Castrol. Subsequent events, possibly two or three years in the future, will tell if he made the right choice.

There are many other factors off the track which are all part of becoming a professional driver who is moving up from Formula 3 to Formula 2 and then on to Formula 1. For someone with enormous natural ability such as Fangio or Moss, Clark or Stewart, the road to the top can be relatively easy. But perhaps only two or three drivers of that calibre are born every decade. The rest have to come up the hard way, using their skill at the wheel of a racing car, not to mention similar talents for impressing the people at the top, making the right decisions at the right time and so on, as well as immense determination and the ability to shrug off setbacks.

Nowadays many drivers are very mindful of their public image and employ specialist public relations companies to assist with publicising their talents and generally making sure that their names are kept in the news as often as possible.

Obviously if you are going to make the top you have got to have a great amount of natural talent (and in some cases money to buy the right drive), so being a nice chap and calling Ken Tyrrell 'sir' whenever you see him is just not enough. With commercial sponsors coming increasingly into racing and expecting the team's drivers to be good salesmen for a product, more importance is being laid on drivers being outward-going personable characters, rather than the silent, quiet types.

Possibly a driver has moved up through the ranks and reached a stage in his career where he realises that, though he is fairly competitive

in say, Formula 2 or Formula 5000, his chances of ever making the 'big time' in Formula 1 racing are remote. Then comes the decision whether he would be better to concentrate on long-distance sports car racing where a good team will employ his talents and pay him well into the bargain. Or possibly he could go to the United States and pick up a lucrative Formula A drive and even a decent Can-Am ride. Such a driver is David Hobbs, who somehow got overlooked by the Formula 1 teams in Europe and thus went to make his racing fortune in America. This decision has proved a very wise one and now David is driving for the top line Roger Penske team and probably earning far more money than are the majority of Formula 1 drivers. Making the right decisions is thus a very important part of every racing driver's career.

How can the young racing driver in Formula Ford make himself noticed by the prospective team managers and sponsors? If you have won a great many races in a particular formula as Vandervell did, the task will not be too difficult. But what if you finished third in the Championship and like four or five other drivers won several important races during the season? Apart from the factors already mentioned, an ambitious driver must show that he has a thoroughly professional attitude to racing. His car should be smartly prepared and he should dress properly in the latest fireproof clothing and generally conduct himself in a professional manner. Stories of wild parties after the race with our prospective hero singing to all and sundry, and doing a strip-tease in the Brands Hatch bar do not, as a rule, go down very well with the people who matter!

One thing is certain, you will never become world champion by sitting in the local pub telling everyone how you broke the lap record for the North Circular road in your MGB and how no one has ever overtaken you on the M1, so really Jackie Stewart had better watch out! To be a racing driver you have first got to race. So sell the MGB, give up drinking and buy a Formula Ford car plus an old van and trailer and prove to the world how good you are. Then it all comes down to handling the power game both on and off the track. □

CHAPTER 10

Hillclimbing

Scenic beauty and split second sport
by Ian Wagstaff

IT MAY surprise many that one of Britain's motor sport venues has been in regular use since 1905. The winner of that event way back at the beginning of the century was E. M. C. Enstone (35 hp Daimler), his winning time being a mere 1m 17.6s. What sort of event was it that Enstone was able to win in such a short time and which in 1971 David Hepworth, in a car of his own design, won in only 29.92 seconds, and where was it?

It was at a place called Shelsley Walsh in Worcestershire and the event was a speed hillclimb. While the object of a motor race is to arrive at the chequered flag before your opponents, the time and speed being largely irrelevant, the object of a hillclimb is for drivers to set out singly on a stretch of road or track which climbs uphill (sometimes very steeply indeed) to reach the top of the hill in a shorter time than any other competitor. Although in Europe these climbs may stretch for many miles, British hills are normally much shorter, mainly 1000 yards or less. Indeed one course, Great Auclum in Berkshire, is a mere quarter of a mile in

---

Well over 400 brake horsepower sets all four wheels smoking as David Hepworth roars away from the lights.

length while the longest British hill to have been used in recent times is Tholt-y-Will, which wound its way over a very difficult 3½ miles.

The times for these events are taken from a standing start, the cars breaking an electric beam as they power off the line and again as they cross the finishing line. This starts and halts the stopwatches, so that a very accurate time is recorded, accuracy being essential as the top competitors are often separated by just fractions of a second. It is not so long ago that a device known as a 'hockey stick' was used, being placed in front of one of the car's front wheels: the weight of the car passing over the foot of the aptly named 'stick' (which contained a switch) starting the watches automatically. Many cars now carry a piece of metal mounted on the front which protrudes into the air and ensures that the beam is broken and that their run is not spoilt, this cunning device being named the 'Burt-strut' after the first person to use one, RAC Sprint Champion Patsy Burt.

From a starting area the courses wind their way uphill, often by a most difficult route (Great Auclum has one banked 45 degree bend) and the driver has to fight hard all the way, for with so short a course the times are often extremely close. A missed gearchange, the wrong line or even the loss of a moment's concentration, and the competitor may well drop right down the placings. Perhaps this explains why hillclimb followers are so enthusiastic about their sport. Where else can one see the drivers working so hard and from so close a viewpoint? In a circuit race, one is often well away from the competitors and a driver can relax if his adversaries are some distance from him, but in hillclimbing the driver must work at maximum efficiency all the time if he is to achieve a really fast run.

As a circuit meeting is divided up into a number of different races, so a hillclimb is divided into classes with the fastest car in each class gaining an award. The various organising clubs have their own ideas about how to divide up the entry into competitive classes, but basically there are the usual categories of single seater, sports car and saloons, divided again into engine capacities, sometimes including such special classes as Historic cars. One club even used to include a class reserved for gas turbine powered cars even before the days of the STP, Howmet and Lotus 56B, though there were never any starters! The award which is most eagerly sought after, especially in a non-championship event, is the fastest time of the day, or FTD, as it is known, but to gain this distinction a driver really has to show his skill.

The best type of car to snatch this coveted award has, over the years, often been a matter of contention. Before the war all manner of cars were used, many being specials built only for hillclimbing, giving rise to the term 'Shelsley Special'. Perhaps one of the most famous was John Bolster's 'Bloody Mary', while other such cars were racers making an excursion away from their usual haunts of Brooklands or Donington. After the war there were a number of racing cars on the market with nowhere in Britain to race, so naturally they took to the hills and such cars as the classic ERA became those with which to gain FTD. However, in the early 1950s such men as the late Ken Wharton discovered what was, at the time, the ideal formula for winning a hillclimb. John Cooper had begun to make some very light but rugged rear engined cars for the old 500 cc Formula 3 and when fitted with 1000 cc JAP Speedway engines they proved unbeatable in British hillclimbs for the next decade.

As these cars became too old, there began a short period of experiment before Peter Westbury, now better known as a Formula 2 driver, came up with an idea which caught the imagination of the hillclimb world in the late 1960s. On such short and tricky courses, his idea was to use a car with the engine driving all four wheels at once instead of the usual two, thereby putting more power on to the road. While four-wheel drive (4-WD for short) has so far been a failure in the world of Formula 1, it was a resounding success on the hills. The Ferguson and BRM 4-WD cars were rescued from the circuits and, in addition such hillclimb notables as six times British Champion, Tony Marsh, and David Hepworth built their own 4-WD specials, and the years 1964 to 1969 saw the domination of hillclimbing by the 4-WD car with Hepworth only narrowly missing the Championship again in 1970.

It is a matter for speculation what will become the best kind of car for hillclimbing in the future. There is still a lot of fight left in the 4-WDs but the advent of Formula 5000 has meant that a number of powerful and 'handleable' McLaren M10s have found their way on to the hills. In 1970 it was one of these single seater V8-engined devices, driven by Sir Nick Williamson, which came out on top. In 1971 Sir Nick returned to his old love—a light Brabham with a small engine—this time a Cosworth FVC such as powers most of Britain's successful 2-litre sports cars.

Hillclimbing in Britain really began as a result of the law forbidding road racing in this country. Enthusiasts would then meet on a lonely stretch of road to match their cars! Usually the law turned a blind eye but not always: a sergeant and a dozen constables met competitors on one notable occasion when they arrived at Dashwood Hill on the London-Oxford road. In 1925 the RAC put a stop to speed contests on the public road, and so the hillclimb as we know it today took shape, usually on a park or the drive to a country house. In the early days with only Brooklands, Donington and Crystal Palace where one could watch circuit racing, hillclimbing was one of the leading branches of British motor sport, gaining a short lived domination shortly after the war when there were no circuits at all. The introduction of the airfield kind of circuit dealt hillclimbing a blow from which it has never really fully recovered.

However, in 1948 an award was introduced which was to become the pinnacle of hillclimbing in this country, namely the Shell-RAC Hillclimb Championship which celebrates its Silver Jubilee in 1971. The first winner was Raymond Mays, (well-known for his connections with the BRM Formula 1 cars) in his own ERA. Other famous names on the championship trophy in those early days were Sydney Allard, Dennis Poore and Ken Wharton, the latter winning the Championship four times. Tony Marsh then started his remarkable winning sequence in 1955, 56, 57, 65, 66 and 67, followed by triple Championship winner, Welshman David Boshier-Jones. Other winners have included the brave one-handed David Good, Arthur Owen, Peter Westbury (two titles), Peter Lawson, Hepworth and Williamson.

In 1971 the Championship was spread over 13 rounds held on courses ranging from Bouley Bay in Jersey, to Doune in Scotland. Shelsley, Prescott (near Cheltenham) and Doune all held two rounds while others such as the popular Gurston Down in Wiltshire claimed one each. The fastest ten drivers after the class runs are allowed two extra runs, providing that they have entered for the RAC Championship. It is these runs alone that count for points, ten being awarded for fastest man, nine for second and so on down to one point for tenth place. An extra bonus point is awarded to anyone breaking the hill record, the Champion at the end of the year often having quite a few of these bonus points in his tally. The Shell Leaders Championship has recently been introduced, points being awarded to the fastest Championship entrants in each class. This is meant to encourage those with the skill but not necessarily the machinery to win the RAC series: no driver can enter for both championships in one year. Another series fast gaining popularity is the BARC Championship. Sponsored by Castrol since 1969 and run at BARC organised events throughout the country, points in this series depend on whether one can beat a 'bogey' time set for one's class and by how much. Other clubs like the Bugatti Owners Club, who run the Prescott climb, and the 500 Owners Association, who cater for the old Formula 3 cars of the 1950s also run their own championships.

Like their mountaineering counterparts, the hillclimbers will continue to ascend hills if for no better reason than that they are there. However, the spirit of competition is strong, (and the atmosphere friendly) with entries becoming even more interesting as the years go by. Most people will find a hill within 50 miles of their home, ranging from Wiscombe Park in Devon to Harwood up in Yorkshire. So there is really no excuse for anyone to miss out on the hillclimb world. Perhaps hillclimbing is not given the publicity it deserves, but with a good commentator (and most of them are good), and fine weather, a splendid day's entertainment is assured. ☐

Left: Split second reactions are a vital asset!

Below: This massive Itala demonstrates that you'll see all sorts of machinery at a hillclimb.

CHAPTER 11

Autocross

Go sideways young man!
by Peter Noad

FUN IN motoring sport is directly proportional to the amount of sideways motion which can be imparted to a car, and the ease (apparent or real) with which control can be lost. This is a fundamental principle applicable to driving and spectating. Now, if you race on slippery grass or mud instead of tarmac, it is a whole lot easier and cheaper to go sideways (and/or lose control). You can even do it in an 850 Mini or an old Ford Popular. This is what autocross is about and why it has grown to become one of the most widely supported types of event in every motor club's calendar.

Autocross was the first of the off-road speed events, being originally devised about 1947. The more recent variations such as rallycross, daylight

stage rallies, rallypoint, and sandocross all stem from the basic autocross concept, and make similar demands on car and driver, although the regulations differ.

It began with trials, which are untimed battles against the country's geography and climate to see if a car can get from A uphill to B. The transition to autocross started when they decided to see not just *if*, but also *how quickly* a car could complete the section. It was then simply a case of turning round, coming back again and timing the complete circuits, and thus autocross had been invented.

Apparently in the early days clubs did things much their own way and made up rules to suit the occasion—like an autoscramble in and out of some woods with both cars and motorbikes competing! In similar style another event had about 30 cars driven by organisers and spectators 'trying out the course' (ie they had a race!) during the lunch interval.

The RAC would get very upset about this kind of thing now, and autocross has regulations which control the course, the cars and the drivers. The number of cars which may start together depends on the dimensions of the course, and there must be plenty of space between the course and obstacles like trees, ditches and spectators.

As with all types of motoring sport there are thoroughly laid down safety requirements, and both the cars and course are inspected by RAC appointed officials.

A typical autocross course will be a half mile or so circuit marked out in a big field, defined by flags stuck in the ground. If drivers hit the flags they get a penalty added to their time and if they go off the course completely—like taking a short cut for instance—they are disqualified.

A run consists of two or three laps and competitors will have several runs. Usually it is their best run only which counts in the results, although in some events aggregate time is taken.

Regardless of how many cars start together, each is individually timed and it is the driver with the fastest time who wins. Technically it isn't a race and that is why the name of the game is speed event, instead of race, In fact it's better than a race since the winner has to keep going flat out.

John Bevan constructed and drove this Naveb Special to the national title in 1970, just one of the many victories that this inexpensive device has scored using a mid-mounted Lotus-Ford Twin Cam engine of nearly 1.8-litres.

even if he's comfortably ahead of the second man, because he has to try for a time that's faster than the winner of the next 'race'.

Cars compete in classes and score points towards championships— such as the Castrol-BTRDA Clubman's Autocross Championship, the RAC Championship, and various sponsored regional championships. Sponsorship of autocross really started with the Player's No 6 Championship, which ran from 1966 to 1970, and it was this which played a major part in boosting autocross to its present level of popularity, and developing the spectator appeal, with extra attractions such as team relay races and knock-out competitions, plus gorgeous girls to present the prizes! The classes vary slightly between different championship series, and they're sometimes changed when a manufacturer introduces a new car that becomes popular for autocross. This is in order to keep an even distribution of competitors in each class. Generally you can expect to see separate classes for front drive saloons, front engine/rear drive saloons, rear engined saloons, sports cars, and specials, with sub-divisions for engine capacity where there are large entries.

Tyre developments and the use of limited slip differentials tend to outweigh any advantages in engine/drive configuration, and it is not easy to predict which class will produce the fastest times. It could be practically any type of car—a Cooper S, Escort Twin Cam, VW, TVR, Elan, or a special. The skill with which it is modified, prepared and driven have far more significance than the name of the factory which produced the original car.

The winning Mini might have a Ford engine, the Escort might have independent rear suspension, the VW might have a Porsche engine, and so on. It all adds up to a lot of interesting machinery representing individual ideas rather than a stereotyped formula.

Special trials cars featured in the early events but these were a bit top heavy and not very stable at speed, so a new breed of autocross specials developed. The most ambitious of these is a twin engined car called Bufi-Mowog, built by Tony Fisher. It has a Cooper S engine in the front and a supercharged British Leyland 1100 in the back. The front engine has a manual gearbox and the rear engine has automatic transmission to avoid the problems which two gear levers would bring!

As well as the challenges of obtaining power and grip (which apply throughout the entire spectrum of motorised sport), autocross poses other problems which test the ingenuity of competitors. Visibility for instance:

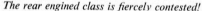

The rear engined class is fiercely contested!

Apart from winning two rallycross championships, Hugh Wheldon's pretty handy in a field as well.

the screen gets instantly plastered with clinging mud and if you can't see out it is rather difficult to stay on course. So autocross cars appear with three gallon screen washers, and various adaptations of pressurised insecticide sprayers and marine bilge pumps, or alternatively perspex screens with Venetian blind slats, and perspex deflector fences on the bonnet.

A successful autocross car has the strength and traction of a rally car, combined with the power and light weight of a conventional racer.

Driving in autocross requires a rather special technique, particularly when the car is pointing at about 90 degrees to the direction of travel and at least one wheel (often three or four wheels) are off the ground! The car is deliberately set into a sideways attitude so that traction from the driving wheels helps to counteract centrifugal force in a corner. With the rear wheels sliding out it responds more quickly and will swing from one direction to another faster than it would if the front wheels were slipping away from the chosen course.

Any car will both understeer (front wheel skid) and oversteer (rear wheel skid) on an autocross surface. Understeer leads to going straight on— either running wide on to the loose porridgy part of the track which wastes time, or right off the course. And an excess of oversteer will end in a spin. Keeping a balance between spinning off and straightening off requires practice and very quick reactions. The technique varies with different types of car. With front wheel drive, putting the power on promotes understeer, and lifting off or braking promotes oversteer. With rear wheel drive, applying power exaggerates whatever was happening before, and removing the power tends to diminish the current effect and bring on the opposite behaviour.

The best line through a corner is dictated by the surface, and time may be lost by using the full width of the track if this puts the car on a softer, looser area (less traction and more drag). Overtaking can often be done by tempting one's opponent to go into a corner too fast so that he runs wide and you can overtake coming out of the corner.

Autocross is certainly entertaining—both for those who do it and those who watch it. A competitive car can often be built up for £200–£300, so this is one of the cheapest ways of jumping into motor sport. ☐

CHAPTER 12

Rallycross

The TV sport of millions
by Jeremy Walton

IF THE SIGHT of four cars leaping through the air and sploshing through mud makes you happy then, like some five million television viewers on winter Saturday afternoons, you will certainly enjoy watching rallycross. This relatively new sport began in its present form back in 1966 when an Independent Television company held an experimental event at Lydden Hill race circuit near Dover in Kent. Since then ITV have maintained an interest in this somewhat grubby and typically British activity, although the BBC are popularly reckoned to attract most viewers with a Championship series now based at Lydden Hill, ITV having moved up to Cadwell Park Circuit near Horncastle in Lincolnshire. A third, untelevised, series of rallycross events is usually held at Croft Autodrome near Darlington in County Durham, a site also used by ITV in the past.

As the name suggests, rallycross is a combination of rallying and autocross, though the cars are usually more like racing saloons with

Left: Sometimes rallycross is a sunny sport, so here Peter Harper's smart Imp and Barry Lee's Escort make for the proverbial hay, pursued by the ever-popular Mini-Cooper S types.
Above: Brian Chatfield's spattered face reflects normal rallycross conditions quite fairly!

raised suspension in order to clear the bumps, and knobbly tyres (though racing tyres are sometimes used in dry conditions) to gain the maximum amount of grip on the rough 'agricultural' surface. All three of these permanent rallycross circuits are arranged so that a maximum of four cars start on a tarmac surface and then alternate between such terrain as chalk, (which, when wet, is more treacherous than ice), mud and grass. Sometimes all four cars will be racing frantically for the finish line, when they hit a hummock, so that a driver must possess the skill of being able to overtake whilst airborne !

The rules have gradually evolved to the point where the ITV series is run on the original basis of three runs, added together to give a total timed result. The BBC series also has three timed runs, but here the winner is decided on the fastest single run. The only other significant difference between northern and southern rallycrossing has been that at Lydden Hill, cars with four-wheel drive start five seconds behind their opponents, whereas at Cadwell Park no such handicap is applied. Because rallycross has become so popular, (it has been known to attract more viewers than the other two great British pastimes, horse racing and football) a number of large companies have given financial help to the organisers enabling prize money to be more attractive. Often they also offer competitors practical assistance in the form of free supplies of their particular product or perhaps a hot cup of coffee on a freezing snowbound day. Probably the best known rallycross sponsors are W.D. & H.O. Wills at Lydden Hill and Castrol at Cadwell Park.

Whilst giving credit to those that televise and provide the backing for these events, it would be wrong to leave out the individuals and organisations who have refined the art of presenting and organising rallycross so that it pleases both the spectators at the circuit and those at home watching it on television. BBC Rallycross events are organised by Thames Estuary Automobile Club (TEAC) and the organisation for ITV events is shared among a number of clubs and individuals, chief of which are the Lincoln and District Motor Club, two officials from the Kentish Border Car Club (Messrs Bud Smith and Dick Mullis, who have been associated with rallycross since its beginnings, as has Bob Reed the ITV producer) and personnel from Castrol.

The early days of rallycross featured a wider variety of cars than are usually present today. Inevitably the drivers have found out which cars are most capable of winning and have put their hard earned money into such vehicles. For the factory, or factory-backed teams, the problem is to produce a competitive and recognisable example of that company's cars. The biggest 'works' efforts in recent years have come from Ford, using Capris and Escorts, versus British Leyland with a vast assortment of likely and some unlikely cars, (even the odd sedate Rover 3500) and Minis of every conceivable type, including those fitted with four-wheel drive. A surprise winner on some occasions in the past has been Chrysler UK with the original Rootes designed Sunbeam Imp, but a recent non-production increase in engine capacity and power has rather spoilt the Imp's reliability record, so that Ford tend to win on the tracks where there are no penalties for using their four-wheel drive 3-litre Capris. On the other hand British Leyland Minis—sometimes in the hands of genuine amateurs —often win where four-wheel drive cars are penalised. This is only a general guide to what the horse racing follower would call 'form', since mechanical trouble, or perhaps an unexpectedly wet day, can introduce unknown drivers into the top ten placings by the end of the day.

In the north the organisers think along more traditional rallycross lines, with the pleasing result that genuine rally cars driven by the top 'pilots' (a suitable term, I can assure you!) will appear in an event scheduled to take place soon after the finish of the RAC rally. This means that with luck one can see foreign cars such as the Lancia, Datsun and Alpine-Renault competing against our best machines. For instance a factory-backed DAF Coupe with four-wheel drive and nearly three times its original horsepower appears regularly at Cadwell Park, along with a very successful Volvo 122S five seater saloon belonging to a York garage, so it is no wonder that 5000 people or more will brave the weather to see what the TV company may not have time to show.

Watching the cars bucking round a rallycross track will probably either make you envious or sorry for those inside their Minis, Escorts, Imps or Capris, but there is no doubt that it is a most exhilarating way of spending a weekend. The best cars are able to accelerate from a standstill to 60 mph in well under 10 seconds, and 60 mph feels more like double that speed when the seat is trying to make contact with your head, and the engine is braying madly *and* shaking the stark metal box in which you are sitting. Fastest of all the cars in a straight line are the works Capris usually driven by Roger Clark, his brother Stan and Rod Chapman. Clark's Capri is geared so that it will not exceed 100 mph, but the acceleration up to that speed via the 252 bhp extracted from its six cylinder vee engine is phenomenal, the four-wheel drive system making sure that most of that power reaches the ground. Recently a four-wheel drive Mini with 120 bhp and weighing rather less than the Capri, succeeded in leaving Roger Clark behind when Brian Chatfield gave this interesting Mini its first competition outing!

At present there are three really fast Ford Escorts. One is the works-backed car of John Taylor fitted with a 'World Cup' 1.8 litre engine, the second is Ron Douglas with an oversize Twin Cam engined version and the third is that British rally hope for the future, Chris Sclater, also with 1.8 litres but this time using a Cosworth BDA engine. On muddy days the 'works assisted' Mini-Cooper S types of Hugh Wheldon and 'Jumping' Jeff Williamson will probably be quicker than the Escorts, although there are a host of 'Minimen' with enormous driving skill yet limited finances who can always be relied on to finish well up in the final order. Men such as Don Gilham, Tony Skelton, Pip Carrotte, Gerry Braithwaite, Gary Streat, Mike Hill, David Angel and Stuart Brown.

Other driver and car combinations worth watching out for are 'Griff' Griffiths (driving a VW 'Beetle' saloon with a 2-litre Porsche racing engine giving 160 bhp); 'Mad' Dan Grewer in the Volvo entered by K Cars of York; the highly experienced Peter Harper and former autocrosser John Homewood in Harper-built Sunbeam Imps. Harper's 1.1 litre engine gives over 110 bhp while Homewood's 1 litre pushes out 100 bhp! Both these Imps are very well prepared, contrasting with some other rallycross steeds which have become a trifle battered after a couple of seasons' harsh contact with both mother earth and other competitors!

At present rallycross can be seen most of the year round, although the emphasis is on the winter series at Croft, Cadwell Park and Lydden Hill. However, the British Automobile Racing Club usually organise three rallycross events during the summer at Lydden Hill. Normally these take place over a Bank Holiday weekend and full details can be found by looking in the Forthcoming Events section of *Motoring News*. ☐

Left: This is what happens if you don't fit good screen washers . . .

Below: The mighty works Ford Capri of Roger Clark stirs up the Lydden mud and snow.

CHAPTER 13

Sprints, slaloms & autotests

Man and machine against the clock
by Peter Noad

SPRINTING really comes in three shapes. Firstly there's the straight line drag sprint (usually over a quarter mile course) catering for extremely specialised 'dragsters', which are dealt with more fully in chapter 17. Then there are circuit sprints which consist of two or three laps of a racing circuit. At these you will see fairly normal road cars, normal racing machinery, and abnormal specials. The third variation is a sprint on an artificial course using marker cones to define the route.

If the route wiggles in and out of the marker cones the event is generally called a slalom, and a penalty of five or ten seconds is given for touching a marker. Like hillclimbing these sports are run against the clock, cars setting off singly—except in the case of drag racing.

A slalom is probably the most interesting of the sprint variants, since it puts emphasis on manoeuvrability rather than ultimate straight line acceleration. The chicanes (artificial corners) and wiggles between markers are approached at up to 80 mph and the careful and accurate judgment of braking in order to swerve through narrow gaps with only a few inches to spare is the real essence of slaloming. It is also a good test of the stability of a car in conditions more relevant to everyday motoring than circuit racing!

Sprints and slaloms usually take place on disused airfields, where there is a good firm surface. Sprint driving requires more precision than most types of motoring sport. The target is a perfect run without a single hundredth of a second being wasted. Perfect start, perfect gear changes and perfect cornering. This is where sprinting differs from rally driving or autocrossing in which one has to deal with unpredictable varying conditions—or racing where there are other cars on the course. The sprint driver has the course all to himself, he has the car set up exactly as he wants it, with correct tyre pressures, fuel level and so on, and he knows he must cover the course in the shortest possible time measured in hundredths of a second! Even placing the car a few inches away from the correct position at the start could make the difference between winning and losing an event.

Competitors usually have several practice runs followed by two or three competitive runs, although it is only their best time which counts in the results. An experienced driver will progressively improve his time with each run as he takes note of places where he can gain a few hundredths of a second by small alterations to his cornering line or gear change point.

Sprints provide the opportunity to drive—and to watch being driven—cars that are not often seen competing at race meetings. These range from standard road cars through to single seater racers made redundant by changes over the years in the racing formulae, plus 'one-off' specials.

The standard cars, whilst obviously not heading for the Fastest Time of Day (FTD) award, do at least make for interesting comparisons with their relative road test figures published in the motoring magazines. Overall fastest time usually becomes a battle between such diverse machinery as David Render's Ford Twin Cam powered Fiat 600, maybe a single seater Vixen Formula 4, a V8 engined Ginetta, a hairy F5000 single seater, and Gerry Marshall's Viva GT. The differing nature of the courses, from the open spaces of Silverstone to the tight twists of a slalom at Santa Pod, make for close competition for class winning points in the various regional championships.

Sprints and slaloms come under the regulations for speed events and, of course, there are appropriate safety requirements. For instance, competitors have to pay special attention to fireproof bulkheads, oil breathers, throttle return springs, ignition switch identification, and cars are always scrutineered for safety in the same manner as for a race meeting.

Autotests bear a resemblance to scaled down slaloms with part of the course covered in reverse gear. They are not specifically 'speed events', but nevertheless the object is still to cover the course as fast as possible. An autotest basically has to be less than 200 yards in length to qualify for the somewhat relaxed safety regulations—such as the wearing of crash helmets being optional and the presence of ambulances not being essential. Maximum speeds are less than 40 mph but the concentration of manoeuvres, including spectacular spin turns, make for challenging and exciting motoring.

An autotest meeting usually consists of 10 or 12 tests involving gyrating 360 degrees around marker cones, stopping and restarting from lines, reversing through narrow gaps and similar manoeuvres. The routes are presented to the drivers as diagrams which they have to memorize before performing the test, doing everything in the correct sequence, as

Winner of the Castrol/BTRDA Autotest Championship in 1970 was Morris Bishop, driving his unique four-wheel steering Mobi One.

Spectacular antics from standard saloons are all part of the sport.

---

fast as possible, without touching the markers or overshooting lines. No practising is allowed and every mistake incurs a penalty or loss of time.

Spin turns are contrived when it is necessary for the car to change direction from forward to reverse, or the other way round. The aim is that the car should never be 'parked' during the test, but should be kept on the move, even when changing from forward to reverse!

Handbrake turns are employed when going forwards, both for a U turn or 360 degree loop round a marker, and for swopping ends to continue in reverse. The technique is different for front wheel drive and rear wheel drive, but the principle is to lock the rear wheels and slide the tail of the car. Accurate timing and co-ordination of the controls is needed to make a neat turn, otherwise the car slides wildly in all directions thus losing time but amusing spectators and frustrating the driver.

Reverse spins are used to rotate the car through 180 degrees whilst travelling nonstop on a line from A to B. When reversing at high speed it is possible to throw the front end around and, if you change gear at the right moment and twiddle the steering correctly, the car instantly swops ends, to continue in the same direction but facing the other way. If you do it badly you end up with a broken gearbox and if you do it Very Badly you finish upside down, so this is strictly one for the experts only! However it really is exhilarating, and saves about 15 seconds compared with a straightforward three point turn. Perhaps the most spectacular example of this technique is if the last part of a test is completed in reverse, but the car has to stop on the finish line facing forwards. Here the autotest driver comes flying backwards towards the finish line, travelling at about 30 mph in reverse, and at the very last moment throws the car round to a standstill

facing the correct way on the finish line, without even having to engage a forward gear: and, it is to be hoped, without demolishing the timing equipment!

An autotest probably demands more concentration combined with physical effort than any other motor sport. Each test is completed in something like 30 seconds, but there may be a dozen manoeuvres in that time each requiring lock to lock turns of the steering, instant gear changes and pulls on the handbrake.

Classes for autotests are based on size of car, usually the wheelbase, rather than engine size. Obviously it is quicker to wiggle a 10 ft Mini between markers 15 ft apart than it is a 14 ft 11 in family saloon. Autotest specials have been constructed which are only about 6 ft long and have 'fiddle' handbrakes so that each rear wheel can be locked separately or, as in the case of Morris Bishop's Mobi One, steering on all four wheels! Specials usually have a handicap of 5% on their times and this makes for close competition with the Cooper S types and BLMC Sprites and Midgets which are, as a rule, the fastest of the production cars. Other makes which, in the right hands, can be very successful are Volkswagens and Ford Escorts. Modifications are directed at improving the handbrake, tightening the turning circle and preventing stalling, rather than developing ultimate engine power. Suspension modifications to prevent the car turning over are desirable in some cases, and strong transmission is needed to survive repeated violent stops and starts.

Autotest venues can be anything from a seaside promenade to a factory carpark or disused airfield. The major championships are the Castrol-BTRDA Flather Star and the RAC Autotest Championship, both with about 20 qualifying events around the country, and there's one international autotest, the Ken Wharton Memorial team event, which for several years has been won by Irish drivers. □

Lean any way you like, but don't stop if you want to win an award.

CHAPTER 14

Trials

The art of ascending the impossible!
by Roger Willis

IT IS six o'clock on a Sunday morning in November. The alarm clock rings and as I open one eye I remember it's time to get up and off to the John Bull Trophy Trial. Trials, or to give them their official RAC title, Fully Sporting Trials, are one form of motor sport which can be enjoyed by the older enthusiast at very little cost. All one needs is a car which complies with the RAC Trials Car Formula, (a good one can be bought for about £350), some means of towing it to events, and the enthusiasm to drive up muddy hills in all weathers.

The whole idea of trials driving is to 'maintain unassisted forward motion' to the top of a hill, or 'section' as it is called. Each section is marked either in ascending or descending order, the winner being the driver who scores the most points, if the scoring is in ascending order, or the least points if it is calculated on descending order. Each car carries a passenger, known as a 'bouncer', whose job it is to bounce up and down in his seat, or place his weight over the rear wheels so as to stop them spinning. As bouncers are often either wives or girlfriends, this goes a long way to making trials one of the most sociable forms of motor sport.

A trials car is one built specifically for this sport. By far the best known make is the 'Cannon', built by Mike Cannon at his farm in Kent. Mike will supply an open body/chassis unit which is made of tubular steel with

CASTROL GUIDE TO MOTORING SPORT

According to the author one needs, 'enthusiasm to drive up muddy hills in all weathers'; the agility of a Jack-in-the-box is also an asset!

aluminium panelling, but the only moving parts he supplies are the 'fiddle brakes'. These are two independent handbrakes, one connected to each rear wheel which, when applied, can stop the rear wheels from spinning, and which will also slide the rear end of the car round under power. 'Fiddle brakes' are mounted either inside the car, between the driver and passenger, or outside the car on the driver's side so that he can operate them with his right hand whilst steering with his left. Cannon will also supply two seat cushions, but the rest of the mechanical parts you must supply yourself.

Still the most popular engine in trials is the 10 horsepower Ford E93A unit, although some BMC 1300 and Renault 1600 engines are now beginning to appear. As the engine power must all be at low engine rpm (incidentally, they never get out of first gear on a section) it is not necessary to spend a small fortune on engine modifications.

As a dynamo is not needed, the most popular extra is an electric Kenlowe cooling fan, which is necessary because a normal fan and dynamo arrangement would take power from the engine. The gearbox, which is usually used with the engine to help in slowing down, will suffice in production form. Front suspension and steering (the car *must* have a good steering lock) can be found in a good breaker's yard. A Ford rear axle (without a limited slip differential) can be purchased cheaply, as can an hydraulic braking system.

The next expense is wheels and tyres. Unlike racing and rallying, there is no need for expensive specialised wheels. A pair of pre-war Ford wire wheels are fine for the front, but steel ones for the rear are advisable. This is because there is virtually no limit to how low the rear tyre pressure may be run, so it is essential to bolt tyres and tubes on to the rims. Rear wheels of 17 inches diameter were popular but they are now becoming hard to get, thus the regulation size has dropped to 15 inches. The front tyres should be of conventional crossply construction, though rear tyres may be of the 'town and country' type.

You can use your road car for trials as well, and preparation is minimal compared with other branches of the sport.

Having built a car, the next problem is transporting it to the various trials venues. Driving it on the road is not practical. When, at the tender age of 17, I asked my insurance company to cover me for taking my car on the road from one group of sections to another, they tried to interest me in a fly-fishing policy! Thus a trailer is required. One can be built from an old caravan chassis quite cheaply, or the car can be towed using an 'A' bracket round the front suspension and steering.

Most trials are held on a Sunday, so an early start is inevitable although usually the more affluent stay the previous night at a convenient hostelry. The first thing to do on arriving at a venue is sign on. This entails producing your competition licence (obtainable from the RAC Competition Department, 31 Belgrave Square, London SW1 at a cost of £1.50) and motor club membership card. Having removed the car from the trailer (it is surprising how many people try and drive their cars off without unfastening them completely!) the next job is to get it passed by the scrutineers. This is usually a pretty painless although very necessary operation; they just check the steering and foot brakes and shake the wheels to make sure they are not going to fall off.

Once all the cars are through scrutineering, the trial can begin. There are usually ten or twelve sections and each will be attempted two or three times. Often one half of the competitors attempt the first hills first and the other half the last hills first, or the even numbers will try the first hills and the odd numbers the last hills. This is to even things out because it will be possible for the early cars to 'clean' (no loss of marks) some of the sections but as more and more cars attempt them, the more muddy and difficult they become.

What comprises a trials section? Really it's a case of anything goes. They usually start off on the level (the car must be stationary at the start) but they can then go up, down and around to suit the terrain. Trees, boulders and other natural hazards are all fair game and the odd river thrown in adds to the excitement. Once a car starts a section it must try to keep going to the top. If it stops, the marks are scored according to where the rear wheels have come to rest. A section is usually 8 or 9 feet wide and the driver must keep inside the section all the time, though there is no time limit laid down. Today all the sections must be in one area without the cars using the public highway, so tow cars are used to attend the local public house at lunchtime, where chatting and swapping of yarns takes place. There are usually fewer sections in the afternoon because of failing light. Once the cars are safely back on their trailers and the crews have cleaned the mud off themselves, they either go back to the 'local' for the prize giving, or home to clean the car.

Production car trials work very much the same way, except that the cars must be run in capacity classes, and they are then split again into front wheel drive and rear wheel drive models. The sections for production car trials tend to be wider and have less natural obstacles in the way, but the sight of a VW or Austin 1300 with smoke pouring from its tyres as it fights for grip on the wet grass is still entertaining. A 'bouncer' can be carried, as can rear seat passengers, (providing they are over 6 years old). Rear tyre pressures have to be slightly higher or else the tyres may roll off their rims.

Whether Sporting or Production Car Trials, the sport enthrals many hundreds of people who find this an enjoyable way to spend a Sunday. □

CHAPTER 15

Racing Vintage Historic cars

by W. Boddy

TO A CONSIDERABLE extent *Motor Sport* magazine can claim to have started the sport of racing in motor cars representative of a more heroic age. At just about the time when the Veteran Car Club of Great Britain was being formed to look after the truly historic automotive heirlooms, Kent Karslake, stockbroker and motoring historian, wrote an innocent article in the aforesaid monthly journal, asking where the old racing cars had gone. This led to several of them coming to light in obscure garages and country hide-outs, Karslake taking advantage of this to commence his fascinating series of 'Veteran Types' articles.

It was the interest thus unleashed which had significant repercussions some years after, the Vintage Sports Car Club being formed in 1934 to cater for those who felt that the then current new sports models, cars which suffered perhaps from the prevailing financial slump, were but parodies for the 30/98 Vauxhalls, 3-litre Bentleys, Anzani Frazer Nashes, 12/50 Alvises and the like of an earlier decade.

For a few years the VSCC, fast gathering momentum and influence,

You can see the drivers at work in the older cars; here a GP Bugatti makes the best of an engine capacity deficit to hold off that pursuing Bentley.

was content to organise trials, speed hillclimbs and races for pre 1931 motor cars of sporting demeanour. Then it occurred to the VSCC committee that equally deserving of preservation, and even more exciting to race, were those pre-Kaiser war racing cars, about which Karslake was enthusing in print. So an Edwardian category was formed and we were treated to the unforgettable spectacle of motor cars such as Clutton's 1908 12-litre Grand Prix Itala, Nash's 1912 15-litre GP Lorraine-Dietrich, Heal's 1910 10-litre Fiat, Morris' 1914 21-litre Benz and Lycett's Alfonso Hispano Suiza doing battle at places such as Donington Park, Prescott and the Crystal Palace.

This cult of not only the enormous and thunderous, but also the smaller pre-1915 cars, grew and was taken under the wing of both VSCC and VCC, by mutual consent. After another war had been weathered, the VSCC decided that the attraction of its race meetings at Silverstone, Oulton Park and Castle Combe (later replaced by Thruxton) would be enhanced, and history preserved, if Post-War, or Historic, racing cars were allowed to take part. These were defined as cars over 12 years old which have front-mounted engines, thus preserving an active interest in classics such as Maserati 250F, Lotus 16, Cooper-Bristol, Connaught, Alfa, certain Ferraris, and so on, together with certain 'specials' of this age built for competition, while excluding later rear engined Formula 1 and 2 cars built more flimsily to later road clinging demands, and in which the drivers lay down to dice so that they could not be seen working away to retain control. Anyway, such cars could be seen in big races or at the meetings of other clubs.

Thus were some of the most exciting, nostalgic and historically significant racing cars not only preserved for posterity but also seen in spirited action several times each year. Remember that VSCC rules already encouraged the *Pre-War* racing cars such as the famous ERAs, Alfa Romeos, Bugattis, Sunbeams, Altas and the like.

What the VSCC will not do is to open its ranks to post-war sports/racing cars, though this the re-formed Frazer Nash Club decided to do, and consequently races for Healey Silverstones, DB Aston Martins, post chain drive Frazer Nashes, Jaguar XK, C- and D-types and so on, are also on the calendar organised by the Historic Sports Car Club.

To attend a meeting where the Pre-War and Historic racing cars compete is to recapture the sights, sounds and smells, along with the thrills, which make racing at Brooklands and Donington a cherished memory. The drivers of such cars race for fun, not finance, for any returns competitors get are of a slender 'part-expenses' nature. If their cars are original, they experience the same level of speed, acceleration, braking and road-holding (or the lack of it) that their counterparts behind the wheels of equivalent cars experienced thirty or more years ago. They enjoy, with the onlookers, unique fascinations such as the scream of superchargers, the rumble of multi-cylinder units like aero-engines, a hard bouncy ride on cord bound cart springs, and the sense of controlling their priceless machines on a high level in a cockpit from which elbows can protrude!

In the interest of safety some modifications may be desirable, in the form of hydraulic in place of cable or rod brakes, larger tyres, strut-type dampers, fireproof engine/cockpit bulkheads, and chassis frames and so on being crack-tested. Some owners of old racing cars may tune them, in respect of both engine and chassis, in an endeavour to uplift their

competition potential. Others, fearful of wrecking irreplaceable cylinder blocks and crankshafts, limit the engine speed of their ancient power units to below those used when such cars were new and the Birkins, Chirons, Nuvolaris and Mays of yesterday were racing them.

Although the bigger races held for this wide divergence of the older motor-cars are scratch events, unfair domination on the part of those with the faster and/or more durable cars is overcome by inserting in the VSCC programmes a supporting series of shorter handicaps, in which the start advantages are doled out on the basis of known performance, a system which worked well at Brooklands for about a quarter of a century. It should be understood that not only the Pre-War and Historic racing cars and so-called 'Edwardian' machinery are to be seen racing at VSCC meetings, but that its entry lists also feature those pre-1931 cars which form the bulk of this club's 6000 membership, and also later cars which it dubs 'Post-War Thoroughbreds'. This is a clumsy but essentially applicable title defining certain cars of the 1931–1940 period, selected by the committee as eligible for driving (as distinct from full) membership, thus broadening the scope of the movement without permitting the entry of mass produced, 'tin box' cars, which, in any case, have clubs and one-make organisations specifically supporting them.

Thus at a VSCC race meeting you have all manner of cars from past years racing together. Where else would you see starting grids filled with Chummy and Ulster Austin Sevens, Riley Brooklands and Sprite, 3, 4½, 6½ and 8-litre Bentleys, Monza and *Monoposto* Alfa Romeos, all the versions (not to mention re-engined examples) of 'Chain Gang' Frazer Nash, Hyper Lea-Francis, Alvises from 12/50 to Speed 25 and 4.3-litre, Derby Bentleys, OMs, GNs and so on?

The more recently introduced JCB Excavator Historic Championship caters for both Historic sports cars as referred to above and Historic

92

Left: Neil Corner has an awe-inspiring collection of motor cars, one of the most successful being this GP Aston Martin DBR1 of the late 1950s.
Above: This Mercedes W125 single seater has recently been restored to its former glory by Colin Crabbe.

racing cars, on a class basis, with races at various circuits as part of the larger race meetings.

It is all the greatest, good natured fun, yet thrilling into the bargain, because the tyres which cars like 1934/36 ERAs use in the 1970s, provided by a provident department of the Dunlop Rubber Company, (without whose supplies of obsolete sizes vintage and veteran activities outside museums would cease forthwith) have the benefit of modern racing rubber mixes, so that the old cars corner faster today than when they were new. Perhaps, too, racing driver prowess has progressed down the years!

A VSCC Silverstone, Oulton Park or Prescott hillclimb is by all standards a thoroughly worthwhile and satisfying happening. It would be invidious to describe the splendid cars which can be seen thereat, and impossible to list them all in the space of this one chapter. Some which come to mind are Neil Corner's 1959 GP Aston Martin, 1936 ex-Raymond Mays' 2-litre ERA and 1925 Sunbeam Tiger V12, the Hon Patrick Lindsay's 24-litre V12 Napier-Railton, holder of the Brooklands lap record, and his Multi-Union which nearly raised it, Kenneth Neve's 1914 TT Humber on correct size tyres, the 1914 and 1922 TT Sunbeams, Philip Mann's rebuilt 1914 French GP-winning Mercedes, Ron Barker's 1908 Napier 6-cylinder, the many Type 35 Bugattis and 1½-litre ERAs in immaculate order and the very fast Maserati 250Fs can be seen. The cult of Edwardian, Vintage and Historic racing has spread to the Continent, and is now a thriving sport, in spite of the rarity of the competing cars and the cost of repairing them if they blow-up—casting just a replacement cylinder block can cost in the region of £500! ☐

The rear-engined Alpine-Renault is one of the quickest rally cars today.

CHAPTER 16

Rallying

The rugged sport
by Geraint Phillips

TO SOME PEOPLE the word rallying signifies a rowdy political demonstration in Trafalgar Square; to others it may mean a theological gathering on the gentle lawns of a country vicarage. Some would say it is a meet of clanking traction engines, perhaps on the occasion of a village carnival. A few would even get within the broad margins of truth and suggest that a rally is an excuse for owners of ancient vehicles to drive their beloved possessions in convoy. However the sort of rallying we want to discuss is packed with action as otherwise reasonable men (and a few women) prove their ability and cars against the elements, each other and the all-important clock.

Because the cars are often spread out don't think for a minute that rallying is boring to watch, for in truth the sight of specially prepared family saloons (and a few rear engine two-seaters) howling through the often bumpy special stages with all four wheels airborne, or in complete broadside power slides, spraying out mud and stones, is something not to be missed. A great feature of rallying is that it is an all-weather sport (providing you are hardy enough to stand around in the prevailing climate!) over all sorts of surfaces so that the cars frequently appear to be out of control. On some stages speeds of up to 110 mph will be reached, and the subsequent spectacle of the driver trying to take the next potholed, off-camber, curve is worth almost any creature discomfort.

Rallying demands virility and endurance, but it is one of the most satisfying sports of the twentieth century and, at the same time, the finest technical test bed available to the motor industry. Success is not easily achieved, so whilst car manufacturers have a perfect right to crow about it when their products win, the participants themselves have the unique exhilaration provided by journeys along unmade tracks at speeds sometimes ten times greater than those at which the mythical Mr Average would dare to venture!

Motor car racing dates back almost to the days of the first car, for man's sporting ingenuity was such that the competitive potential of the new contrivance was soon realised. First there were races from point to point, but these eventually gave way to races on closed circuits, and that is probably when certain enthusiasts became a little bored with the repetition of it all. They wanted something a little more adventurous, something which combined the requirements of a race with the need for physical endurance, mental exertion and a lively sense of humour.

So the rally was born. In the early days they were hardly more than excuses for socialising, but as machines became more efficient and the men who drove them more expert, it became the fashion to introduce as many natural obstacles as possible into the sport. Modern motor racing is all smooth ferro-concrete and tarmacadam, with every obstacle giving the slightest hint of danger removed or sterilised with clinical ruthlessness. Rallying is fortunately free from such artificial doctorings. Indeed, natural hazards are welcomed by the versatile rally driver. He treats ice and snow as life-long friends; he welcomes the thunderclouds; he may not like fog or choking dust, but he'll do his best in the circumstances.

The cars used in current international competition are as special as the people who drive and navigate them. The redoubtable men of the Ford works team will be seen either in highly tuned and strengthened Escorts or in the sleek GT70, a two-seater racing car with a mid-mounted engine which has been designed to rally against the German Porsche 911S (rear engine, steel bodied two-seater), or Porsche 914/6 also with a steel sports body, but mid engined, the hugely successful French Alpine-Renault A110 with glassfibre body and rear engine, steel bodied mass production models such as the sporting Lancia 1.6 Rallye from Italy, (Fiat models such as the 124 Coupé are often seen as well) and the bulky but shatteringly fast Japanese Datsun 240Z sports car. From the list you can see that British honours in international events of recent years have mainly been in the hands of the American-owned Ford Motor Company! British Leyland works entries appeared in the World Cup Rally, taking second place, but it has been some years since the men of Abingdon scored an International victory, their competition department being officially closed—though the right parts to convert a British Leyland car for rallying are still available from Abingdon. The same is true at present of the Chrysler concern's competition activities based in Coventry (they won the London-Sydney marathon with a Hillman Hunter), but not of course of Ford, who stock vast mountains of parts with their Advanced Vehicle Operation at Aveley in Essex.

The whole object of a rally is to get from one place to another within a certain time. Cars do not race against each other, for they are segregated by a staggered start. The adversary is the clock, not the competitors behind or in front. On public roads, all the normal traffic laws have to be observed, and there is even additional legislation directed at rally people which everyday road users do not have to observe. The Motor Vehicles (Competitions and Trials) Regulations demand, for instance, that no rally shall require an *average* speed between two points greater than 30 miles per hour, an exception being a route which includes a run along a motorway. There are even extra rules imposed by the RAC which go far beyond the provisions of government legislation. These not only protect the sport's participants but also the general public.

The budding rally driver has to start at the bottom. Shrewd as they may be in finding short cuts, rally drivers have not yet discovered one which leads to the top of the ladder. The order of things could roughly be described as follows: join a motor club (there are hundreds from which to choose); take part in its closed rallies; when sufficiently experienced, accept the invitations of other clubs to tackle restricted events; move up to compete in national grade rallies; when sure of one's competence, embark on international events, in Britain at first and then abroad. Each stage of this progression demands a licence of one kind or another, from the club membership card which is needed for closed events to the full international competition licence needed for top grade events. When starting from the bottom, one must prove experience before the licence for the next grade can be issued by the RAC—a system which operates in much the same way as that for racing and other forms of motoring sport.

Unlike racing, rallying is an activity which demands the undivided concentrations of two people, both of whom are in the car at the same time. One drives, and the other navigates, to put it as simply as possible. A car may be driven at an incredibly high speed; if it is not going in the right direction its occupants might just as well have stayed at home. Hence the need for a navigator! Usually the organisers of a club rally indicate the route by means of a list of Ordnance Survey map references, though spot heights and other landmarks are sometimes used.

For short rallies (200 miles and less) the term navigator applies to the man (or woman) who sits in the passenger's seat with a one-inch-to-the-mile Ordnance Survey map on his knees, telling the driver where to go and warning him in advance of bad bends, steep descents and the various other hazards which are indicated on these splendid maps. Indeed, the good navigator keeps up a running commentary so that the driver is constantly aware of what to expect around the next corner or over the next blind crest. A sort of human radar set, if you like. Of course, horse-drawn hay carts and cattle on their way to the milking shed are beyond even the cartographic skills of Her Majesty's map makers, so the driver has always to keep something in reserve!

In a rally of 200 miles there can be anything up to 50 time controls

Above: Ford's GT70 could be the rally car of the future.

Left: The 1.9 Opel Kadett is capable of great things, but too much optimism can lead to this situation.

Below: The works Ford Escorts have been fitted with a number of engines, but the Twin Cam and RS versions are the most successful.

where competitors must stop so that a record may be made of their arrival times. Many ingenious methods have been devised to minimise delay at time controls, the best known being the Targa Timing system, so called because it was introduced by the organisers of a British rally called the Targa Rusticana. It relies on a system whereby the clocks at each time control are so adjusted that a competitor running 'on time' throughout a rally would encounter the same reading on every one. The winner is the man who has lost the least time at these controls, which demands fast and steady driving and accurate navigation. In larger events, speed tests may also be incorporated in the route.

Experience counts for much in the realm of navigation, a measure of a navigator's capabilities (or perhaps the length of his tooth) can often be the degree to which he has recorded on his maps such additional information which is not on the mint copy. Information such as the location of gates across the road, the depth of fords, the degree of roughness of un-surfaced roads, the severity of bends, the paths of new roads and various other items.

In an international competition, where drivers of many nationalities gather in one country, it is obviously unfair to make use of a system where-by familiarity with the terrain and the degree to which one's maps are marked with extra information provide an advantage. Furthermore, it has become undesirable to have the meat of a tough international rally on the congested roads of Britain. Unlike other countries, we cannot have the benefit of temporary road closures for rallying (even though the cycling fraternity somehow manages this for cycle racing), so all the hard, fast rallying of the major events in Britain has taken to private roads the surface of which usually has much in common with a farm track: the public highway is used merely as a means of getting from one private road to the next.

Above: The SAAB can be a real flyer in the right hands!

Right: This Triumph 2.5PI finished second on the World Cup Rally in the hands of Brian Culcheth/Johnstone Syer. The same pair now use it for rallies in Britain.

Nowadays, British international rallies such as the RAC Rally, the Scottish Rally, the Welsh Rally and the Circuit of Ireland, provide their competitors with route books in the 'Tulip' style. So called because it was first used by the organisers of the Tulip Rally in Holland, this system uses a series of little diagrams each representing a junction, with the distances between them accurately given to the nearest hundredth of a mile. Thus, with an accurate distance recorder, a rally crew can traverse a route by going from diagram to diagram without having to open a map at all. Of course, the advantage of the 'human radar set' is lost, because the navigator cannot warn the driver of what is around the next bend, but at the gentle, cruising speeds employed on public roads this is of little consequence.

Sections on private roads are known as 'special stages'. In Britain, most of them are provided by roads through our State Forests. They have no metalled surface, and are generally of compacted earth and stones, firm beneath but loose on the surface. To drive over them at the high speeds demanded by present-day rallies requires an amount of skill which only a few possess. Each special stage, anything from 5 to 25 miles long (though much longer in some other countries), has a fixed target time, and penalties are awarded at the rate of one point per second in excess of that time. It is very rare indeed for a competitor to beat the target time. In other countries, there are often no target times, the contest being on a scratch basis with penalties equal to the actual time taken.

It has already been said that true navigators are required only in events of 200 miles or less, where the sole means of defining a route is by maps. On longer events, a different kind of skill is required, although the efficient co-driver should never forget his map reading ability. In the rally regulations there is a rule which forbids a rally competitor to drive continuously for more than 200 miles without a break. Therefore it is necessary that the driver should change places with his partner occasionally, hence the term co-driver. The number-one driver naturally tackles all the special stages, but the co-driver must also be able to drive quickly and safely, just as the driver should also be able to take on the duties of his mate if necessary. After all, both of them are going to need sleep at some stage or other in a long event spanning several days.

Practising, and the notes which competitors make during practice sessions have given rise to a highly sophisticated form of human radar called 'pace notes'. They are far more accurate, and far quicker to transmit from co-driver to driver than information read out from a map. Every bend, camber, surface, brow, incline and any other hazard is committed to paper in a shorthand form. There are many variations on this shorthand, but the basic essentials are that it should be completely familiar to both crew men and should be translated into cryptic monosyllables, quick to speak but impossible to confuse. If there is any failure in communication, the result is likely to be a spectacular accident.

For instance, full throttle is read as 'flat', and the codes used by most competitors are full of such terms. Pace notes have been so developed by British rally crews that many foreigners, whose languages are perhaps more tongue-twisting than English, use English when reading pace notes simply because it is quicker to read. This applies particularly to Scandinavians, many of whom have rallied with British co-drivers and have passed the system on to their friends at home.

Unlike map reading on open public roads, the use of pace notes on roads closed to all other traffic, (where special stages take place) makes it possible for a skilled driver to drive faster and safer, for he knows that he will meet no opposing traffic and can therefore use the whole width of the road. Even in thick fog, a pair of competitors who have been rallying together for some time and have become attuned to each other, can drive at virtually undiminished speed. Such skills are not easily acquired, but you will find that the world's best drivers and co-drivers had their humble beginnings in club rallying and progressed steadily up the scale.

To start rallying is not at all difficult. All one needs, really, is an inexpensive motor car like a Mini or an Escort and various odds and ends to go with it. But like all other activities there is a natural desire to progress from better to best, and sooner or later will come the need for costly modifications. Until that time comes, be content with a slow start. It is a hard, demanding, exciting but immensely satisfying sport at all its levels, and it is possible to have just as much fun and enjoyment from a one-night rally in the Welsh mountains as from a Monte or an Alpine. Never forget that one rally does not turn you into a Roger Clark overnight, for even he took time to get off the bottom rung.

As you progress, cast your eyes at the championship of your own club and then that of your area association. When you feel that you are ready, tackle some of the qualifiers of the national championships—one is run by the RAC for drivers only and another by *Motoring News* in conjunction with Castrol for both drivers and navigators. Beyond that, if you have ambitions to become a professional you will obviously set your sights on

Above: The Porsche 911S has proved its versatility with a number of fine international rally victories.

Right: Threat from the East as a Datsun 1600 leaps on Safari. The same firm has won the African event with their 240Z sports car.

the classic rallies qualifying for the International Championships—the Monte, Thousand Lakes, Alpine, Acropolis and Swedish rallies, for instance. Before venturing on any of these, it is worth remembering that non-championship events frequently offer just as much value for lower outlay, the prize money can often be higher and more accessible, and the professionals may be competing elsewhere. The FIA Year Book is invaluable to the aspiring rally competitor, for it lists all the world's international events with the addresses of their organisers. It is published by Patrick Stephens Ltd at 9 Ely Place, London EC1N 6SQ.

Finally, a word about the debt which civilisation owes to rallying. Whatever some cynics may say, the motor car is a vital part of our lives, and its development, particularly in recent years, owes much to lessons learned on special stages. All too often we have heard that 'racing improves the breed'; nowadays the claim is that this part or that is 'rally proved', which is probably nearer the mark. Sophisticated racing suspensions have little connection with those of road-going passenger cars. The same can be said of the highly specialised rubber compounds used in the manufacture of racing tyres. In rallying, road-going products often see the light of day for the first time, and many a suspension, tyre tread design, engine mounting, headlamp reflector, seat belt layout, windscreen glass, instrument panel, body strengthener, and a host of other modifications owe their present efficiency to tests carried out by rally drivers in the course of their competitions.

There is an unfortunate tendency nowadays to look upon any success as being occasioned by the motor car, he who drives it being given just a little smaller slice of the publicity cake. In racing it is possible for a good car to be the making of its driver, whereas in rallying the accent is fairly and squarely on the shoulders of the competitors. Many a rally driver has produced unexpected publicity for the makers of his chosen car. Who would have thought that, in 1970, John Bloxham could have taken his mother's Fiat on a championship rally and gone home the winner? Or that in 1959 Ken Piper could have won a national rally in a 'three-wheeler' Messerschmitt? Those who have previously been winners of the *Motoring News*/Castrol Rally Championship are listed below. Today's top drivers (who have more than one old-timer among them) can be seen on most championship events these days, and to find out when these take place one only has to open the pages of *Motoring News*. □

MOTORING NEWS RALLY CHAMPIONSHIP PAST WINNERS

	DRIVERS	NAVIGATORS
1961	Bill Bengry	Brian Melia
1962	Tony Fisher	Brian Melia
1963	Reg McBride	Don Barrow
1964	Reg McBride	Don Barrow
1965	Gerald Bloom	Alan Taylor
1966	Malcolm Gibbs	Randal Morgan
1967	Jim Bullough	Don Barrow
1968	Colin Malkin	John Brown
1969	John Bloxham	Richard Harper
1970	Jim Bullough	Don Barrow

CHAPTER 17

Miscellaneous motoring sport

Some other ways of watching four-wheel sport
by Jeremy Walton

WHEN COMPILING a book of this nature it is all too easy to devote all the space to the branches of the sport that people know best. Mention motor sport to most people and they immediately think of Graham Hill or Jackie Stewart whistling around a track with slot-car precision. However thousands of spectators, or potential competitors, prefer to watch cars which put the accent on action. Dragsters billowing smoke from the rear wheels as they bellow away to exceed 200 mph in 440 yards, old cars jostling in a tightly packed bunch around a stadium oval or on grass, and ordinary road cars mixing it with the autocross specials for a meeting held entirely on a coastal resort's beach—all these offshoots of our sport have their own fanatical following.

Perhaps the most neglected offshoot of all is Go-Karting, a sport which has given single seater racing many promising stars for the future. Like drag racing, karting history traces back to America, both sports being imported into this country by American servicemen in Britain. Drag racing is by far the older-established of the two but karting has become

Hot Rods such as Barry Lee's Escort please the crowds with their fiery racing at stadium ovals.

CASTROL GUIDE TO MOTORING SPORT

Drag racing is full of spectacular 'burnouts', such as this one by Nick Colbert.

very popular in Britain, mainly from the competitor's point of view as it provides such cheap yet skilled sport.

The majority of karting goes unseen by large crowds, relying on little known local tracks, though occasionally spectators at Silverstone or Brands Hatch will see the wheel to wheel slipstreaming antics of the bigger 250 cc karts, which average over 80 mph on Silverstone Grand Prix circuit. Although these larger engined karts are probably best known (there is an annual World Championship for such devices), the novice can build, or buy secondhand, a far simpler machine which will require no gearchanges. There are classes catering for anything from 100 cc engines, using a centrifugal clutch like that on a lawnmower to give a maximum speed of 45 mph, up to the 250 cc machines capable of easily exceeding 100 mph. For further details of this sport, which has produced such notables as Bev Bond, Colin Vandervell and Roger Williamson, contact the RAC or Karting magazine (published monthly) at the addresses given at the end of the book.

Drag racing is the art of covering a quarter mile faster than the competitor who starts alongside you, the cars usually starting in pairs. The time it takes for a car to cover the quarter mile of straight asphalt, and the speed at which it crosses the finishing line, are a relevant guide to the best competitors, but it is the chap streaking past that finishing line first who will be declared the winner. The victor of a class may face a number of opponents on a knockout basis, the leader going on to face a new challenge. Cars are normally signalled to start by a 'Christmas tree' of lights (one set per car) which count down by individual bulbs to a green 'go' signal: if a car jumps the start by even a split second the lamps will flash red on the side of the offending machine. Having triggered off the electronic timing equipment, the powerful American V8-powered saloons or the long ladder-like 'rails' may paw the air with their front wheels, whilst the rear wheels shod with 'slicks' (tyres with no tread pattern) momentarily fade beneath wreathing rubber smoke.

A British 'rail' will probably have only one V8 engine of 7-litres plus, burning an exotic mixture of nitromethane, alcohol and methanol, to return a quarter mile time of just over 7 seconds (200 mph terminal speed!).

In the USA times of less than 6½ seconds and speeds over 230 mph are not unknown. As a comparison you will find that it takes a really potent sports car of the Ferrari/Lamborghini ilk some 6½ seconds to launch itself from rest to 60 mph!

The British Drag Racing and Hot Rod Association (BDRHRA) control the sport in this country using the only permanent drag strip in Europe as a base, namely Santa Pod Raceway in Northamptonshire. The Association do promote events elsewhere, as do the National Drag Racing Club (NDRC). Apart from the straightforward 'rails' with their tubular chassis and open wheeler layout, you can expect to see every conceivable permutation of saloon car with the most unlikely power units. As an example it is quite common practice in England to insert a Jaguar engine into an old 'sit up and beg' Ford Popular: another variation on the saloon car theme is to fit a glassfibre body, which looks like a popular family car, over a pure dragster chassis and engine. In America they have the latter art superbly brought to a climax in the so called 'Funny Cars', these 1500 horsepower giants being little slower than the open 'rails'.

One of the most important benefits that drag racing offers is that a competitor can use his everyday transport to gain an understanding of the lightning reflexes needed to wheelspin the car on its way, without incurring the dreaded red light. In fact British drag racing looks to be something like ten years behind its American parent, but recent injections of much needed money have brought a lot more colourful machinery for spectators to watch.

Above: Paul Fletcher shows that Go-Karts can powerslide with a front wheel airborne.

Left: Topline stock car driver Geoff Goddard grapples with a Superstock at Aldershot.

Right: A 'funny car' has a plastic body hiding a full blooded dragster underneath.

Sand racing is classed by the RAC as a Speed Event, and as such comes under much the same rules and regulations as those which control auto-cross. Cars may start in pairs or groups of four, according to the track. The standard of racing will be similar to autocross and rallycross, though the cars do not generally spend much time in the air, unless the driver has made a mistake in his estimation of cornering speed! The majority of British sand racing takes place either at Ainsdale Beach, Southport, near Liverpool (promoted by Liverpool Motor Club), or at Weston-Super-Mare in Somerset, organised by that seaside resort's own motor club.

What sort of cars are you likely to see throwing up the sand? The answer is that the majority will be mass produced saloon cars like the Ford Escort, Capri, British Leyland Minis of all engine capacities, and so on. Both the saloon cars and modified versions of the same breed have to conform to the RAC Vehicle Regulations, which also apply to all the other branches of the sport approved by the RAC. If you are on holiday in the Channel Islands at any time, study the local papers carefully, for the chances are that you will find a sand race meeting advertised near to where you are staying.

Jalopy or grass track four wheel activity is held in this country but is outside the jurisdiction of the RAC, as is the majority of stock car or stadium racing. The fact that the RAC does not approve usually means that the vehicles and track do not comply with the RAC's ideas on safety equipment: this does not mean it is unsafe to watch or take part in such

sports, quite the reverse in most cases, for the organisers (who are making reasonable profits and wish life to continue in the same way) enforce their own realistic standards on competitors and the tracks which they use. There are exceptions though, so choose your vantage point with care!

Stock cars demand the most skill from their drivers and the most admiration from the crowds at places such as Ipswich, Walthamstow, White City and Aldershot stadiums. Starting in groups of around 30 cars, with the fastest drivers at the back, the cars may cover a pair of 25 lap heats of a quarter mile tarmac oval and a longer final, so it is not a sport for weaklings. The cars are sturdy rather than beautiful, conforming to rules laid down either by the Spedeworth organisation or the British Stock Car Board of Control (authorised by BRISCA). A car can be built for £200 or less, plus a lot of hard work constructing it and finding second hand parts.

Unlike club racing or rallying, the driver is paid for appearing, thus some are professional entertainers earning something like the price we quoted for the car, but per week! Against this one has to remember the accidents (though the object is no longer merely to crash, the accent now being firmly on leading to the finish—there's more money to be earned that way!) and the chances of blowing up one of the production based power units. Taking into account the costs of attending a meeting, most competitors still manage to make a little money on their racing and provide an awesome spectacle as they slide their way round in one huge colourful pack, glimmering in the overhead arc lamps. Facilities at these stadiums up and down the country are bound to vary, though writing from personal experience in the home counties I would say that most open air circuits could take a lesson from the covered grandstands and fine eating amenities offered to the spectator at a stadium.

Stock cars have been known to appear at Brands Hatch and other open air circuits where RAC approval is needed, and there has been little difficulty in gaining approval for such a venture, so long as the cars comply with RAC safety regulations. The same applies to Hot Rods, which translate as rather battered cousins to the saloons one sees at a conventional race meeting. The Midgets, with their 1300 cc engines and single seater configuration, are really like the old upright dirt trackers that trained such American stars as Mario Andretti, Parnelli Jones, A. J. Foyt and the Unsers: the snag is that they don't have the performance of their American counterparts.

Grass track or jalopy racing is far more informal than even the dare devil attitude frequently found in stadiums. The cars are dirt cheap and look it, but they really do provide spills and thrills which are not smiled upon by the RAC. On occasion you will see vehicles without doors, so the Royal Automobile Club's attitude can be understood!

The address of the Car Grasstrack Racing Organisation appears at the back of this book, but it should be stressed that this field sport is now pretty popular in the country and there are clubs whose existence is only known within the area in which they stage events. Compared to autocross the sport is slightly slower, but there are usually more starters, so there is plenty of bodywork bashing to keep boredom at bay.

Of these motoring offshoots that we have discussed, drag racing has the greatest potential for growth (it is *the* motor sport in the USA), but you should also enjoy a trip to a stadium to see the stock cars at play! ☐

No relation to the footballer, just a good example of a well-equipped Formula Ford driver all togged up to go.

CHAPTER 18

How to enter motoring sport

What you need, and why
by Alan Henry

SOONER OR LATER it's almost certain to cross the mind of the enthusiast watching from the public enclosure that it's about time he stopped spectating and started participating. With so many differing branches of the sport he is bound to find something to cater for his taste and pocket: circuit racing, rallying, hillclimbs, autocross, rallycross . . . the list goes on and on. This chapter has therefore been planned to give some guidance to the newcomer keen to make a start and to point out some of the decisions he will have to take.

No matter in which field you want to try your luck, the first thing to obtain is the appropriate competition licence from the RAC. For circuit racing a special medical certificate must be issued by your doctor. This involves a fairly rigorous check up and includes an eyesight test, but understandably the RAC must be careful not to issue licences to anyone who suffers from any illness which might mean he would be a danger to fellow competitors. For all branches of the sport, a full driving licence is needed, but the medical certificate will only be required for circuit racing and for International rallying. Some small local club events will be exempt from RAC requirements, but these form the exception to the rule.

The novice driver will be issued with a Restricted licence, renewable at the end of each year, which permits one to compete in straightforward club race meetings. If the competitor performs to the satisfaction of the RAC steward present, then his race record card (on the back of the licence) will be signed. A minimum of six signatures is required for upgrading to a National, and further signatures for an International licence. No matter which class of the sport the novice has his eyes on, much thought at an early stage should be given to the choice of safety equipment. The first and probably most obvious compulsory piece of protection is the crash helmet. Development of crash helmets has been very extensive over the past few years and current safety standards offer a high degree of protection. If you are planning to drive an open car of any sort then an all-enveloping helmet which gives protection to the face is a good bet. It may cost substantially more than the more usual 'open face' helmet, though £35 for a 'Bell Star' is cheap compared with the cost of replacing your jaw! All crash helmets must conform to British Standard Specification 2495— the 'kite mark' is printed inside on the lining—and there's a good range on the market from about £12 to £40.

The next thing to think about if you use an open-face helmet is the question of goggles: there is a lot of argument as to whether they are preferable to a vizor, but generally speaking tight fitting goggles can be considered to be best for vision and comfort in dry weather. Bubble visors which snap on to the press studs on the front of a helmet are ideal for deflecting the water in really heavy rain, the snag being that they do have a tendency to mist up.

It's not so long ago that you could go down to Goodwood or some such club circuit and watch amateur drivers racing in nothing more than short-sleeved cotton shirts and casual trousers. If you turned up in that

sort of garb at a club meeting nowadays, although you wouldn't be turned away, you would hardly be welcomed. It's just not worth skimping on a set of fireproof overalls which could well mean the difference between stepping out of a crash unhurt, or suffering painful burns and their consequences.

There are a bewildering variety of flameproof racing suits currently on the market, but it is worth referring to the results of some recent tests carried out by the Jim Clark Foundation before making a choice. In these extensive experiments were carried out on the effect of fire on various protective substances. The materials eventually recommended were the Bellcor, Durette or Fypro overalls for outside protection, with Taslan textured Nomex, Kynol or ordinary Nomex knit worn below, *plus* ordinary underwear. Remember that in the event of a fire it is vital to protect your face (balaclava helmet), hands (gauntlet gloves) and feet (fireproof socks). Although it sounds like a lot of expense (about £50 to be fully equipped) you may well have cause to be very thankful you paid out that money.

Once you've acquired all your equipment and appropriate licence, the next step is to decide how best to make an active start. If you are keen to go circuit racing then the first thing to do is join a club which regularly organises such meetings. The British Racing and Sports Car Club (BRSCC) and the British Automobile Racing Club (BARC) between them hold meetings at several circuits in Britain and they keep their members supplied with up to the minute information on the racing scene. These two clubs are the biggest, but hundreds of other clubs are listed in the RAC 'blue book', with which you will be supplied when you apply for a competition licence. Think about it carefully and study the merits of going to one of the two well established racing schools if you are not really sure that you have an aptitude for racing. Motor Racing Stables, which

Left: Crystal Palace is not the place to find out that the car will not go round corners! David Brodie's leading Escort is an example of top preparation that can only help at scrutineering time.

Above: Racing can be expensive!

Right: They give you all sorts of things to wear if you're a marshal!

Above: Not recommended if you want a signature for your novice licence!

Right: The ultimate target is often to be talking to the tall one of this pair: his name is Ken Tyrrell. His companion is a certain Mr J. Stewart, who seems to be pretty good at this Formula 1 game, so please don't interrupt.

operates from Brands Hatch, and the Snetterton based Jim Russell school have experienced instructors who will tell you frankly whether you stand a chance. After all the schools want to make money—and if you are *that* bad, they will not risk their cars! The average cost of training in the school Formula Ford cars is about £1 per lap and generally you should be able to go right through the school for between £60 and £150 depending on which one you select. In both cases they organise races between their pupils, so you can get on a starting grid for the first time at a fraction of the cost of buying your own car.

There are those who will tell you that this is a waste of money as nobody can teach you to race. This is true, nobody can persuade you to keep your foot on an accelerator pedal for a fraction of a second longer than your reflexes tell you is safe, but they do give you practice in driving a single seater on a race track. If your taste is for rallying then your local motor club is almost bound to belong to one of the area associations which hold an annual rally championship in your region. The chances are that they run autocross meetings as well during summer weekends, and that your club will be invited by neighbouring clubs to compete in other events.

The biggest single investment will of course be your competition car. Now here there is a real danger of going out and buying a load of old uncompetitive rubbish and then not being able to get rid of it when you find out just how unsuitable it is for the sporting job you have in mind.

If you don't like being alone, or simply have insufficient money to buy a car for track use, then rallying may be your best choice. It is, of course, still possible to use your everyday road car for club rallies at the weekend, although when you reach a higher level things get pretty specialised and you will need a proper rally car. There's an abundance of pleasure to be found bouncing round Welsh mountains in the middle of a rainstorm, trying to convince yourself that the bloke you brought along to navigate is in fact a friend! Your car will need a laminated windscreen, seat belts, a sump guard and a roll over cage in addition to the usual rallying accessories such as a tripmeter, a battery of spotlights, some knobbly tubed tyres and the necessary Ordnance Survey maps. Throw in lashings of patience, lots of hot coffee, the ability to change a wheel in the middle of a Scottish forest during a blizzard, and you are nearly half way to becoming a rally driver!

Over the last few years autocross has become a very popular branch of the sport. From the organisational point of view all that is needed is a large grassy field and plenty of enthusiasts willing to bump their way round a makeshift track marked out by flags, starting in pairs. Again this branch has become pretty sophisticated with lots of purpose built specials. although it's still possible to beef up your road car and have a great deal of fun. Rallycross is rather more serious and a special saloon or sports car is necessary if any success is to be achieved. Generally rallycross events are rather rougher, start four cars at once, are certainly faster and run over a mixture of mud, slush or snow covered tarmac. They are supported by factory teams since there is extensive television coverage during the winter, and usually there are generous prize funds going down to tenth place with a chance of picking up trade bonus money as well. If you are good at autocross the chances are that you will do well in rallycross, provided you have a reliable and competitive car.

To gain experience on a circuit and use your normal road car at the same time, there are generally a number of sprint events run at various tracks throughout the year. Usually run over two or three flying laps, four cars run together, but the contest is against the clock and not specifically between competitors on the track (the same principle applies to autocross). A sprint offers the advantage that the novice has only to concentrate on driving round the course as fast as he can without his mind being occupied by avoiding other cars. Similar enjoyment can be obtained from hillclimbing at club level, but be warned that there are some expensive Formula 5000 and even Grand Prix cars being used in the RAC Hill Climb Championship if you should ever venture that far, though as with all categories of motoring sport, there are classes for all sorts of machines.

Once you've sifted through all the problems involved in making a start in this exciting pastime your ambitions may start you on a professional career in motoring sport. Don't be discouraged by possible early failure. Stirling Moss started with a small 500 cc motor cycle engined Cooper at club hillclimbs just after the war, Jim Clark drove his family Sunbeam Talbot in club rallies, and Jacky Ickx drove motor bikes in trials. Jack Brabham served his apprenticeship in dirt track racing (as did Mario Andretti), Emerson Fittipaldi just drove karts, while Graham Hill started his career at, that's right, a racing school! ▯

APPENDIX 1

Where to go

A guide to Great Britain's racing circuits, hillclimbs, sprint courses and stock car tracks

---

THIS SECTION has been planned as a guide to where you can see the particular type of motor sporting competition that most appeals to you. It lists all 18 permanent racing circuits in the United Kingdom (England, Scotland, Wales and Northern Ireland), together with an outline plan of the track and a map showing the approach roads to the circuit. There are also helpful details of where to apply for tickets, the exact geographical location, the track length, the maximum number of cars permitted to start in one race, the type of racing that can be seen and, for those who do not have a car, how to attend by public transport. Subsequent sections also give useful information on the best known hillclimb courses, sprint venues and stock car tracks.

The Forthcoming Events column in *Motoring News* every Thursday will give a reliable guide to what is happening and where, but careful study of a local paper may reveal events to cheer up your weekend.

Aintree

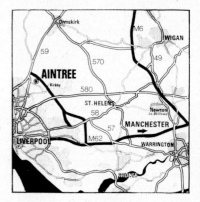

Address:
Aintree Automobile Racing Co Ltd, Racecourse Offices, Liverpool 9.

Telephone:
051 525-3500.

Location:
5 miles north-east of Liverpool, accessible from the Melling Road, by Blue Anchor bridge.

Length:
1.64 miles.
Max no of starters:
18.

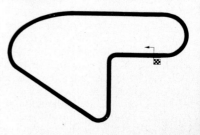

How to get there:
Local bus services in frequent operation from central Liverpool.

Used for:
Club racing; practice days organised by Aintree Circuit.

112

Bishopscourt

Address:
Bishopscourt Airfield, Bishopscourt, Downpatrick, Co Down.

Telephone:
Downpatrick 2351 (race days only).

Location:
3 miles south-west of Strangford, 5 miles east of Downpatrick on unclassified road signposted Ballyhornan.

Length:
2.13 miles.

Max no of starters:
25.

How to get there:
Bus service from Downpatrick to Ballyhornan passes circuit. Timetable enquiries phone Belfast 32355.

Used for:
Club racing.

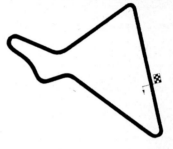

Brands Hatch

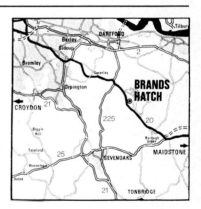

Address:
Brands Hatch Circuit Ltd, Fawkham, Near Dartford, Kent.

Telephone:
West Ash 331.

Location:
20 miles south-east of London on A20, near Farningham.

Length:
Grand Prix circuit, 2.65 miles; Club circuit, 1.24 miles.

Max no of starters:
Grand Prix circuit, 35; Club circuit, 20.

How to get there:
Bus—Greenline 719 from London to Wrotham. For local services telephone Swanley 2075.
Train—from Victoria, Holborn Viaduct, Sevenoaks and south coast to Swanley. Special bus service from Swanley station for major meetings.

Used for:
International, National, Club and stock car racing; also occasionally utilised for karting.

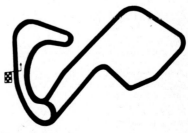

Cadwell Park

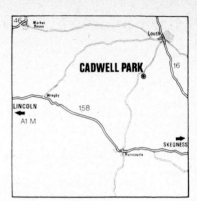

Address:
Chas Wilkinson, Cadwell Manor, Louth, Lincs.

Telephone:
Louth 3779/Stenigot 248/651.

Location:
7 miles north-west of Horncastle on A153, 5 miles south-west of Louth.

Length of circuit:
2.25 miles.

Max no of starters:
22.

How to get there:
Bus—services from Lincoln and Sleaford to Horncastle. From Grimsby, Market Rasen and Lincoln to Louth.

Used for:
International, National and Club racing for cars under 2000 cc. Also stock cars, karting and televised rallycross.

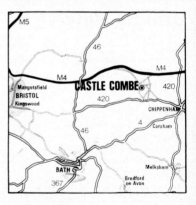

Castle Combe

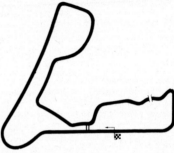

Address:
Castle Combe Circuit, Chippenham, Wilts.

Telephone:
Castle Combe 278; Castle Combe 395 (race and practice days only).

Location:
5 miles north-west of Chippenham on B4039.

Length of circuit:
1.84 miles.

Max no of starters:
20.

How to get there:
Bus—399 service from Bristol to Chippenham.
Train—Chippenham station on Paddington to Bristol line. Timetable enquiries Chippenham 2252.

Used for:
National and Club race meetings.

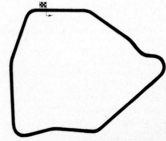

114

Croft Autodrome

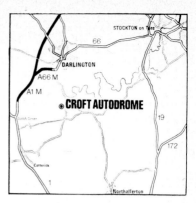

Address:
Croft Autodrome, Croft, Darlington, Co Durham.

Telephone:
Croft 206/659.

Location:
7 miles south of Darlington, 5 miles east of Scotch Corner.

Length of circuit:
1.75 miles

Max no of starters:
24.

How to get there:
Bus—service from Darlington station to circuit. (Weekdays and Bank Holidays 12.23, Sundays 13.15.)
Train—Darlington station from Kings Cross.

Used for:
International and Club racing; also for non-televised rallycross.

Crystal Palace

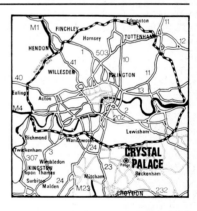

Address:
Crystal Palace Offices, Anerley Hill, London SE19.

Telephone:
01-778 4691.

Location:
South-east London, near Sydenham.

Length of circuit:
1.39 miles.

Max no of starters:
16.

How to get there:
Bus—2, 2B, 3, 12, 49, 63A, 108, 122, 137, 154, 157, 227 services.
Train—Southern Region trains to Crystal Palace, Penge East or Penge West.

Used for:
International and Club racing; also occasional karting.

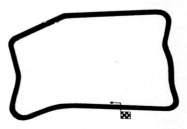

Ingliston

Address:
Scotcircuits Ltd, National Bank Chambers, Duns, Berwicks.

Telephone:
Duns 3724.

Location:
7 miles west of Edinburgh on A8 Glasgow road.

Length of circuit:
1.03 miles.

Max no of starters:
15.

How to get there:
Bus—regular service from Edinburgh.
Train—Waverley station (Edinburgh) from Kings Cross.
Air—1 mile from Edinburgh Airport.

Used for:
National and Club race meetings.

Kirkistown

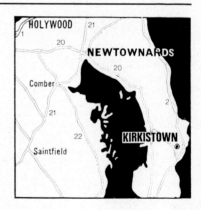

Address:
The Secretary, 500 Motor Racing Club of Ireland, Kirkistown Circuit, Kircubbin, Newtownards, Co Down.

Telephone:
Portavogie 325 (race days only).

Location:
3 miles south-east of Kircubbin on B173.

Length of circuit:
1.53 miles.

Max no of starters:
20.

How to get there:
Bus from Newtownards to Portaferry via Cloughey passes about 1 mile from circuit. Timetable enquiries phone Belfast 32355.

Used for:
National and Club race meetings.

116

Llandow

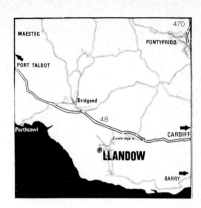

Address:
South Wales Automobile Club, 1-2
Wellington Street, Cardiff.

Telephone:
Cardiff 27240.

Location:
4 miles south-west of Cowbridge, Glam.

Length of circuit:
1.00 mile.

Max no of starters:
18.

How to get there:
Bus—service from Cowbridge to Llantwitmajor.

Used for:
Club race meetings.

Lydden

Address:
William Mark Holdings Ltd, 71 West
Street, Sittingbourne, Kent.

Telephone:
Sittingbourne 72926; Shepherdswell 557
(race days only).

Location:
7 miles south-east of Canterbury, Kent.

Length of circuit:
1.00 mile.

Max no of starters:
14.

How to get there:
Bus—East Kent Line service 15 from
Canterbury. Hourly service.
Train—Shepherdswell on Southern
Region Victoria to Dover.

Used for:
Club races, karting and televised rallycross; also occasional stock car meetings.

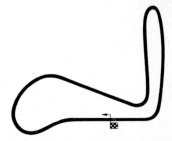

Mallory Park

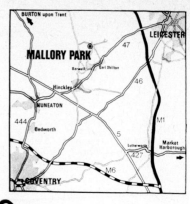

Address:
Mallory Park, Kirkby Mallory, Leics.
Telephone:
Earl Shilton 2631.

Location:
9 miles south-west of Leicester just off
A47.

Length of circuit:
Long circuit 1.35 miles; Club circuit 1.00
mile.

Max no of starters:
Long circuit 20; Club circuit 15.

How to get there:
Bus—688 service from Hinckley to
Kirkby Mallory. 658 service from
Leicester to Earl Shilton.
Train—Leicester station. Timetable en-
quiries to Leicester 29811.

Used for:
International, National and Club racing.

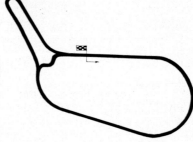

Mondello Park

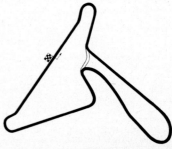

Address:
Motor Racing Circuits Ltd, Mondello
Park, Naas, Co Kildare, Eire.

Telephone:
Dublin 63630; Naas 60151 (race and
practice days only).

Location:
4 miles west of Naas off T5, 20 miles
south-west of Dublin.

Length of circuit:
1.24 miles.

Max no of starters:
16.

How to get there:
Bus—13.00 on race days from Bus Aras,
Dublin, Timetable enquiries to Dublin
47911.
Train—Kildare Town and Newbridge
stations from Dublin, Cork and Limerick.
Timetable enquiries to Dublin 47911.

Used for:
National and Club race meetings.

118

Oulton Park

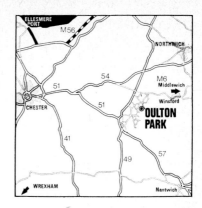

Address:
Cheshire Car Circuit Ltd, Oulton Park, Little Budworth, Tarporley, Cheshire.

Telephone:
Little Budworth 301.

Location:
Near Tarporley off A54.

Length of circuit:
2.75 miles.

Max no of starters:
30.

How to get there:
Bus—North Western Road Car Co services from Manchester, Macclesfield, Warrington and Altrincham to Northwich, then shuttle service to circuit from bus station. Timetable enquiries to Stockport 2213.
Train—Crewe station. Timetable enquiries to Crewe 55123.

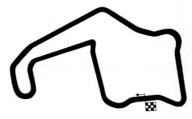

Used for:
International, National and Club racing.

Rufforth

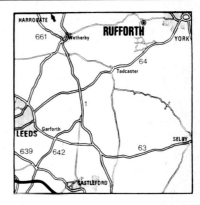

Address:
BRSCC, York House, 21 Park Street, Leeds 1.

Telephone:
Leeds 28659.

Location:
5 miles west of York on B1224.

Length of circuit:
1.7 miles.

Max no of starters:
24.

How to get there:
Bus—Local services from York.
Train—York station, thereafter by bus.

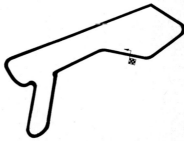

Used for:
Club racing.

Silverstone

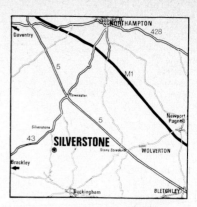

Address:
Silverstone Circuit Ltd, Silverstone, Near Towcester, Northants, NN12 8TN.

Telephone:
Silverstone 271.

Location:
15 miles south-west of Northampton on A43.

Length of circuit:
Grand Prix circuit 2.927 miles, Club circuit 1.608 miles.

Max no of starters:
Grand Prix circuit 36, Club circuit 25.

How to get there:
Bus—345 service from Northampton bus station to Silverstone village.
Train—Northampton station from Euston.

Used for:
International, National and Club racing.

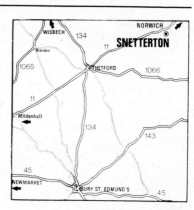

Snetterton

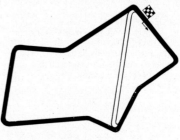

Address:
Snetterton Circuit Ltd, Snetterton, Norwich, NOR 1OX.

Telephone:
Quidenham 303/4.

Location:
10 miles north-east of Thetford, Norfolk on A11.

Length of circuit:
2.71 miles.

Max no of starters:
33.

How to get there:
Bus—12 service from Norwich to Attleborough. Timetable enquiries to Norwich 20491.
Train—Attleborough and Thetford stations on Norwich to Cambridge line. Timetable enquiries to Norwich 20255.

Used for:
International, National and Club racing. Occasional stock car racing.

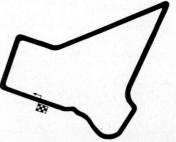

Thruxton

Address:
Thruxton (BARC) Ltd, Thruxton Circuit, near Andover, Hants.

Telephone:
Weyhill 344.

Location:
4 miles west of Andover, on A303.

Length of circuit:
2.356 miles.

Max no of starters:
30.

How to get there:
Bus—Apply to Wilts & Dorset Motor Services Ltd, Bridge Street, Andover (Andover 2339).
Train—Southern Region stations to Andover. Connecting coach service arranged for major meetings.
Coach—Royal Blue Express Coach Services, National House, Queen Street, Exeter (Exeter 74191).

Used for:
International, National and Club racing.

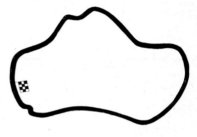

Hillclimb courses

Baitings Dam, Yorks

Location: Blackstone Edge. 5 miles south-west of Sowerby; approach on A58.

Length of course: 410 yds.

Surface: Tarmacadam throughout.

Average width: 11′ 4″.

Principal organisers: Knowldale Car Club; Lancashire Automobile Club; Lancashire and Cheshire Car Club; Spitfire Owners' Club.

Useful address: N. J. Tudor Thomas, Lancashire Automobile Club, 10 Cannon Street, Preston, Lancs.

Barbon Manor, Westmorland

Location: 2¾ miles north-east of Kirkby Lonsdale via A683.

Length of course: 880 yds.

Average gradient: 1 in 12.

Surface: Tarmacadam throughout.

Principal organisers: Westmorland Motor Club.

Useful address: R. Cannon, Westmorland Motor Club, Glenwood, Brigsteer, Nr Kendall, Westmorland.

Bodiam, Sussex

Location: Grounds of New House Farm, Bodiam.

Length of course: 670 yds.

Surface: Tarmacadam throughout.

Principal organisers: Hastings 1066 and East Sussex Car Club.

Useful address: A. G. Bird, East Sussex Car Club, Highview, Battery Hill, Fairlight, Hastings, Sussex.

Brunton, Hants

Location: Off A338, ¼ mile north of Collingbourne Kingston.
Length of course: 585 yds.
Principal organisers: BARC (South West) Centre.
Useful address: E. C. Britten, BARC (South West) Centre, 15 Bournemouth Road, Chandlers Ford, Hants, SO5 3DA.

Cadwell Park, Lincs

Location: 8 miles north-north-east of Horncastle on A 153.
Length of course: 1,400 yds.
Principal organisers: BARC (East Midlands) Centre.
Useful address: J. K. Warrillow, BARC (East Midlands) Centre 101 Station Road, Cropston, Leics.

Castle Howard, Yorks

Location: 5 miles west of Malton via A64, then SP 'Castle Howard'.
Length of course: 580 yds.
Principal organisers: Yorkshire Sports Car Club.
Useful address: P. Croft, Yorkshire Sports Car Club, 56 Reins Road, Rastrick, Brighouse, Yorks.

Craigantlet, Co Down

Location: 8 miles east of Belfast via A20, then SP 'Craigantlet'.
Length of course: 1,833 yds.
Principal organisers: Ulster Automobile Club.
Useful address: W. Kinnear, Ulster Automobile Club, 3 Botanic Avenue, Belfast, BT7 1JG.

Ditcham Hill, Sussex

Location: Off B2146, 3 miles east of Petersfield.
Length of course: 880 yds.
Principal organisers: Chichester Motor Club.
Useful address: Miss J. Dutton, Chichester Motor Club, 75 St Leodegars Way, Hunston, Chichester.

Doune, Perthshire

Location: 1¼ miles west of Doune, SP 'Callander'.
Length of course: 1 mile.
Average width: 12'.
Surface: Hard Bitmac throughout.
Principal organisers: Lothian Car Club.
Useful address: Competition Secretary, Lothian Car Club, Scotia Office Machines 2/4 Castle Terrace, Edinburgh 1.

Fintray House, Aberdeenshire

Location: 8½ miles north-west of Aberdeen via B977 from Dyce.
Length of course: 620 yds.
Average width: 10'.
Surface: Tarmacadam throughout.
Principal organisers: Aberdeen and District Motor Club.
Useful address: Competition Secretary, Aberdeen and District Motor Club, 12 Golden Square, Aberdeen.

Gt Auclum, Berks

Location: 6 miles south-west of Reading.
Length of course: 440 yds.
Average width: 12'.
Surface: Tarmacadam throughout.
Principal organisers: Hants and Berks Motor Club.
Useful address: D. Hogg, Hants and Berks Motor Club, 22 Broadlands Court, Wokingham Road, Bracknell, Berks.

Gurston Down, Wilts

Location: 1 mile west of Broadchalke.
Length of course: 1,160 yds.
Principal organisers: BARC (South West) Centre.
Useful address: M. Norris Hill. BARC (South West) Centre, Wentways, Beauworth, Alresford, Hants.

Harewood, Yorks

Location: Stockton Farm, 7½ miles east-north-east of Leeds.
Length of course: 1,100 yds.
Average width: 13'.
Surface: Dressed tarmacadam throughout.
Principal organisers: BARC (Yorkshire) Centre.
Useful address: M. S. Wilson, BARC (Yorkshire) Centre, Silver Royd House, Leeds, LS12 4QQ.

Hemerdon Hill, Devon

Location: 2¼ miles north-east of Plympton.
Length of course: 440 yds.
Average width: 21'.
Surface: Concrete throughout.
Principal organisers: Plymouth Motor Club.
Useful address: Competition Secretary, Plymouth Motor Club, Raynham Court, Raynham Road, Penlee, Plymouth.

Loton Park, Salop

Location: 8½ miles west of Shrewsbury.
Length of course: 1,475 yds.
Principal organisers: Hagley and District Light Car Club.
Useful address: John H. Dorsett, Hagley and District Light Car Club, Alpha Business Services, Mart Lane, Stourport-on-Severn, Worcs.

Oddicombe, Devon

Location: North-west of Torquay, adjacent to B3199.
Length of course: 750 yds.
Principal organisers: Torbay Motor Club.
Useful address: J. Burgoyne, Torbay Motor Club, Green Pastures, Veille Lane, Shiphay, Torquay.

Olivers Mount, Yorks

Location: 1 mile south of Scarborough via A64.
Length of course: 1,600 yds.
Principal organisers: BARC (Yorkshire) Centre.
Useful address: M. S. Wilson, BARC (Yorkshire) Centre, Silver Royd House, Leeds, LS12 4QQ.

Pontypool, South Wales

Location: Pontypool Park, Glamorgan.
Length of course: 850 yds.
Principal organisers: BARC (South Wales) Centre.

Useful address: N. Jones, BARC (South Wales) Centre, 5 Holywell Road East, Abergavenny, Mons.

Prescott, Glos

Location: 5 miles north-north-east of Cheltenham via A435.
Length of course: 880 yds.
Principal organisers: Bugatti Owners Club.
Useful address: Godfrey Eaton, Bugatti Owners Club, 40 Bartholomew Street, Newbury, Berks.

Scammonden, Yorks

Location: Scammonden Dam, 5 miles west of Huddersfield via A640.
Length of course: 850 yds.
Principal organisers: BARC (Yorkshire) Centre; Huddersfield Motor Club.
Useful address: M. S. Wilson, BARC (Yorkshire) Centre, Silver Royd House, Leeds, LS12 4QQ.

Shelsley Walsh, Worcs

Location: 10 miles west of Worcester via B4204.
Length of course: 1,000 yds.
Average width: 14′.
Surface: Rolled colas and chippings.
Principal organiser: Midland Automobile Club.
Useful address: G. Flewitt, Midland Automobile Club, 4 Vicarage Road, Edgbaston, Birmingham, B15 3ES.

Sprint courses

Ainsdale Beach, Lancs

Location: Ainsdale, Nr Southport.
Length of course: 1 mile.
Average width: 30′.
Surface: Hard sand.
Principal organiser: Liverpool Motor Club.
Useful address: David Aukland, Liverpool Motor Club, 6 Hard Lane, St Helens, Lancs.

Blackbushe, Hants

Location: 2 miles west of Blackwater; approach by A30 from Bagshot.

Length of course: 1,200 yds.
Average width: 30′.
Surface: Asphalt.
Principal organiser: BARC (Surrey) Centre.
Useful address: P. D. Cunnell, BARC (Surrey) Centre, Overdrift, Tower Hill, Dorking, Surrey.

Burtonwood, Lancs

Location: Airfield, 2 miles north-north-west of Warrington.
Length of course: 1.7 miles.
Surface: Mostly tarmac, a little concrete.

Principal organiser: Chester Motor Club.
Useful address: K. Anson, Chester Motor Club, 33 Coniston Drive, Frodsham, Via Warrington, Cheshire.

Crimond, Aberdeen

Location: 8 miles south-east of Fraserburgh, via A952 from Peterhead.
Length of course: 1.4 miles.
Average width: 40′.
Surface: Tarmac.
Principal organiser: Aberdeen and District Motor Club.
Useful address: I. A. Hay, Aberdeen and District Motor Club, 12 Golden Square, Aberdeen, Scotland.

Curborough, Staffs

Location: 2½ miles north-east of Lichfield on unclassified road from A38.
Length of course: 900 yds.
Width: 15′.
Surface: Tarmac.
Principal organiser: Shenstone and District Car Club.
Useful address: M. Finnemore, Shenstone and District Car Club, 3 High Street, Sutton Coldfield, Warwicks.

Duxford, Cambs

Location: 7 miles north of Royston on A505.
Length of course: 1,400 yds.
Principal organisers: Cambridge Car Club; Morgan Sports Car Club; Falcon Motor Club; North London Enthusiasts Car Club.
Useful address: A. J. Scamber, Cambridge Car Club, 26 High Street, Dry Drayton, Cambridge.

Greenham Common, Berks

Location: 2 miles south-east of Newbury, off A34.
Length of course: 1 mile.
Surface: Concrete and tarmac.
Principal organisers: Southsea Motor Club; BMW Owners Club; Jaguar Drivers; East Surrey Motor Club.
Useful address: T. Hellier, Southsea Motor Club, 21 Goodwood Close, Cowplain, Hants.

Milfield, Roxburgh

Location: 6 miles north-west of Wooler on A697.
Length of course: 440 yds.
Principal organiser: Hawick and Border Car and Motor Cycle Club.

Useful address: D. G. Campbell, Hawick and Border Car and Motor Cycle Club, Wilderburn, Galashiels, Selkirk.

Moreton-in-the-Marsh, Glos

Location: 4 miles north of Stow-on-the-Wold, approach via Fosse Way.
Length of course: 1,350 yds.
Surface: Asphalt.
Principal organiser: North Cotswold Motor Club.
Useful address: A. Lapsley, North Cotswold Motor Club, Fujima, Swan Close, Moreton-in-the-Marsh, Glos.

North Weald, Essex

Location: 4 miles north-east of Epping on A122.
Length of course: 440 yds.
Principal organiser: Harrow Car Club.
Useful address: D. Crome, Harrow Car Club, 66 Sherington Avenue, Pinner, HA8 0LT.

Princes Way, Blackpool

Location: Part of the promenade at North Shore, Blackpool.
Length of course: 1,000 yds, with shallow chicane.
Average width: 25′.
Surface: Concrete throughout.
Principal organiser: Longton and District Motor Club.
Useful address: M. Davis, Longton and District Motor Club, 38 Pope Lane, Penwortham, Preston, Lancs.

Santa Pod, Northants

Location: 6 miles south-east of Wellingborough via A509 to Wollaston, then unclassified road.
Length of course: 440 yds.
Surface: Dressed concrete.
Principal organiser: Santa Pod Raceway Ltd
Useful address: 95/97 Martins Road, Shortlands, Bromley, Kent.

St Eval, Cornwall

Location: 4 miles north-west of St Colomb Major; approach via unclassified roads.
Length of course: 1½ miles.
Principal organiser: Newquay Motor Club.
Useful address: B. Lanyon, Newquay Motor Club, 29 Polsue Way, Tresillian, Truro, Cornwall.

Woodvale, Lancs

Location: 5 miles south of Southport off A565.
Length of course: 2.6 miles.
Principal organiser: Lancashire Automobile Club.
Useful address: A. Iddon, Lancashire Automobile Club, 7 Lyndon Avenue, Great Harwood, Blackburn, Lancs.

Yeovilton, Somerset

Location: 5 miles north of Yeovil. Approach from Yeovil via A37 and unclassified road.
Length of course: 870 yds.
Principal organiser: Yeovil Car Club.
Useful address: A. Mansfield, Yeovil Car Club, 2 Summerfield Park Avenue, Ilminster, Somerset.

Stock car racing tracks

Spedeworth Ltd, Aldershot Stadium, Tongham, Farnham, Surrey. Circuits where you can see Spedeworth promoted racing—which include classes for Superstox, Hot Rods, Midgets, Stock Cars, Auto-Spedeway—are as follows:

Aldershot Stadium. Oxenden Road, Tongham, Farnham, Surrey. Spedeworth's headquarters. Easily accessible from London (on the A3), at the foot of the Hog's Back, just outside Guildford. Regular evening meetings during the season on Thursdays and Saturdays, plus Bank Holiday meetings. Good car parks, tarmac surfaced track, clubhouse and bar, one small seating stand.

Arlington Raceway. Just off the A22, 1 mile from Hailsham, Sussex, 7 miles to the London side of Eastbourne. Regular Sunday afternoon meetings during the season. Concrete surfaced track, car park, one small seating stand, refreshments.

Bradford. At time of going to press negotiations were nearing completion for Spedeworth to race on one of Britain's biggest stadiums, situated in Bradford. Racing will take place regularly on Saturday nights during the season. All covered stands.

Cross-in-Hand (Sussex). This attractive and unusual circuit is situated on the A267 Tunbridge Wells-Hailsham Road, at its junction with the A265 near Heathfield. Racing takes place on certain Sundays and Bank Holidays throughout the season. Concrete surfaced track, seating cut into banking, refreshments available, clubroom and bar.

Ipswich Stadium. Situated on Foxhall Heath, with the entrance in Foxhall Road, on the outskirts of Ipswich. Only a short distance from the main A12 Ipswich to Saxmundham road. Racing takes place on many Sunday afternoons and also on some Saturday evenings throughout the season; ¼ mile tarmac surfaced track, clubroom and bar, new covered stand under construction, large car park and camping and caravan facilities.

Matcham's Park. Near Ringwood, Hampshire, within the New Forest. Attractive tarmac surfaced track. Racing on regular Sunday afternoons and Bank Holidays, plus two-day events. The site is the centre of new sports development and motel. Refreshments and large car park.

Newport (Monmouthshire). One of Spedeworth's newest tracks, in South Wales, not far from Cardiff. Racing on regular Saturday evenings. Also plans for further development; all covered stands.

Walthamstow Stadium. Situated in Chingford Road, near the Crooked Billet Public House, on the North Circular Road/Chingford Road roundabout, Walthamstow. Racing takes place on regular Fridays in the season, and also on certain extra holiday meetings as advertised. All covered glass-fronted stands. Restaurants, bars, car parks and children's playground. Tarmac surfaced track.

White City Stadium. In Wood Lane, near Shepherds Bush, London W12. Easily accessible by public transport. Racing on regular Friday nights on ¼ mile tarmac surfaced track. Restaurant, bars, large car park, all covered stands.

Wimbledon Stadium. Situated just a few minutes from Tooting Broadway, London SW17. Racing takes place on regular Saturdays from late February until November. All covered centrally heated stands. Shale/tarmac surfaced track. Bars and restaurants and large car park.

Wisbech Stadium. On the Peterborough Road, between Wisbech and Peterborough. Racing on regular Saturday nights and Bank Holidays throughout the season. Concrete surfaced track. Covered stand, bar, clubhouse, refreshments, car park.

Yarmouth Stadium. Situated in Caister Road, Great Yarmouth, Norfolk. Racing takes place at this holiday stadium on many Tuesdays and Sundays during the season, with extra meetings on some Fridays during the peak holiday period. Tarmac surfaced track, covered stands, bar, refreshments and car park.

The Stock Car Racing Board of Control Ltd, (appointed by the British Stock Car Association, known as 'Brisca'), 232 High Road, London N22 (Tel 01-888 8456/7/8). Circuits where you can see racing in the 'Brisca' manner include:

Aycliffe Stadium. Aycliffe Trading Estate, Co Durham (Tel Aycliffe 2442). 370 yards tarmac surfaced track. Car park, terracing, bars, buffets. Promoters: Apex Promotions Ltd. Manager: Ron Deane Meetings held on Sundays at 3 pm.

Belle Vue Speedway. Hyde Road, Manchester 12 (Tel 061-223 1331). 418 yards of granite surfaced track. Car parks, grandstand, restaurants. Amusements include a park, zoo and dancing. Promoters: Entam Pleasure Parks Ltd. Meetings held on Saturdays and Bank Holidays at 7 pm.

Boston Stadium. Situated in Wyberton, off the A52 Boston to Sleaford Road (Tel Boston 61175). 385 yards of shale surfaced track. Free car parks, grandstand, buffets and bars. Promoter: 'Chick' Woodroffe, 'Linsteads', Orsett Road, Horndon-on-the-Hill, Essex. Meetings held on Saturdays at 7.45 pm.

Brafield Stadium. Brafield on the Green, Northampton—4 miles south-east of Northampton, 4 miles off M1 (Tel Hackleton 206). 435 yards tarmac surfaced track. Car park, grandstands and

buffets. Promoter: John La Trobe. Manager: Graham Guthrie, c/o Post Office, Steventon, Abingdon, Berks. Meetings held on Sundays at 3 pm.

Bristol. Mendip Raceways, Warren's Hill Road, Shipham, near Bristol (Tel Fordingbridge 3030). 380 yards tarmac surfaced track. Car park, terracing and buffets. Promoter: Gerry Dommett, High Street, Fordingbridge, Hants. Meetings held on Sundays at 3 pm.

Coventry Stadium. Rugby Road, Brandon, near Coventry—on the A428 Coventry to Rugby road (Tel Wolston 2395). 380 yards of shale surfaced track. Car parks, grandstand, cover, restaurant, buffets and bars. Promoters: Charles Ochiltree, in association with Midland Sports Stadiums Ltd. Meetings held on Saturdays at 7.30 pm.

Crayford Stadium. Situated in Crayford, Kent, between Dartford and Bexley. 310 yards shale surfaced track. Restaurant, bars, buffets and car park. Promoter: Mike Parker Promotions, 81 Upper Chorlton Road, Manchester 16 (Tel—day Moss Side 3559, night Sale 4008). Meetings held on Fridays at 8 pm.

Harringay Stadium. Green Lanes, Harringay, London N4, near Manor House Tube station (Tel 01-800 3474, office 01-888 8456). 343 yards of tarmac surfaced track. Car park, grandstands, restaurants and bars. Promoter: Stan Hinckley. Meetings held on Good Friday, and Saturdays at 7.45 pm.

Hednesford. Hednesford Hills Raceway, near Brownhills, 20 miles north of Birmingham. Birmingham Office: 163 Bordesley Green Road, Birmingham 9 (Tel 021-772 1060). 440 yards of asphalt surfaced track. Grandstand and free car park. Promoter: Bill Morris. Meetings held on Saturdays at 7.30 pm, Sundays and Holidays at 3 pm.

Kings Lynn Stadium. Saddlebow Road, Kings Lynn, Norfolk (Tel Kings Lynn 3753). 400 yards of shale surfaced track. Free car parks, grandstand and buffets. Promoters: 'Chick' Woodroffe, Promotasport Ltd, 'Linsteads', Orsett Road, Horndon-on-the-Hill, Essex (Tel Orsett 777). Meetings held on Sundays at 3 pm.

Long Eaton Stadium. Station Road, Long Eaton, Nr Nottingham (Tel Long Eaton 2693). 360 yards of shale surfaced track. Car parks, grandstand, licensed club bar, buffets. Promoters: Track-master Promotions, 116 Holme Road, West Bridgford, Nottingham (Tel Nottingham 82993). Meetings held on Good Friday and Saturdays at 7.30 pm.

Nelson. Seed Hill Stadium, Carr Lane, Nelson, Lancs. 350 yards of granite surfaced track. Free car parking. Promoter: Mike Parker Promotions, 81 Upper Chorlton Road, Manchester 16 (Tel—day Moss Side 3559, night Sale 4008). Meetings held on Saturdays at 7.30 pm.

Newton Abbot. The Racecourse, Newton Abbot, Devon (Tel Newton Abbot 2627). 330 yards of tarmac surfaced track. Car parks, grandstand, bars and buffets. Promoter/Manager: Trevor Redmond for Auto Speed Circuits. Meetings held on Holidays, Wednesdays at 7.45 pm.

Rayleigh Stadium. Rayleigh, Essex—on A127, 8 miles from Southend (Tel Rayleigh 71854), 365 yards of shale surfaced track. Free car park, grandstands, bar and buffets. Promoters: 'Chick' Woodroffe, Promotasport Ltd, 'Linsteads', Orsett Road, Horndon-on-the-Hill, Essex (Tel Orsett 777). Meetings held on Good Fridays at 3 pm and Saturdays at 7.45 pm.

Ringwood. Matcham's Park Stadium, Hurn Lane, Ringwood, Hants. 410 yards of tarmac surfaced track. Car park, terracing and buffets. Promoter: Gerry Dommett, Garage, High Street, Fordingbridge, Hants (Tel Fordingbridge 3030). Meetings held on Bank Holidays and Sundays at 3 pm. (Also used by Spedeworth Ltd).

Rochdale. Athletic Ground, Milnrow Road, Rochdale. 417 yards of granite surfaced track. Car parks, grandstand and refreshment bars. Promoters: Entam Pleasure Parks Limited, Hyde Road, Manchester 12 (Tel 061-223 1331). Meetings held on Fridays at 7.15 pm.

St Austell. Cornish Stadium, Par Moor, St Austell, Cornwall (Tel Par 2615). 360 yards of granite tarmac surfaced track. Car parks, grandstands, licensed club and buffets. Promoter/Manager: Trevor Redmond for Auto Speed Circuits. Meetings held on Tuesdays at 7.45 pm.

St Day. United Downs Raceway, St Day, near Redruth, Cornwall. 350 yards of tarmac surfaced track. Car parks, buffets and embankments. Promoter/Manager: Trevor Redmond for Auto Speed Circuits. Meetings held during holidays

Useful names and addresses

British Automobile Racing Club (BARC):
Sutherland House, 5/6 Argyll Street,
London W1 (01-437 2533).

British Drag Racing and Hot Rod Association: Mrs E. Bartlett, 55 West End Court,
West End Lane, Stoke Poges, Bucks
(Farnham Common 2103).

British Jalopy Racing Association: G.
Edmond, 16 Claremount Road,
Gloucester.

**British Motor Racing Marshals Club
(BMRMC):** L. D. Pullen, 1 Willowmead
Close, Ealing, London W5 (01-997 0154).

**British Racing and Sports Car Club
(BRSCC):** Empire House, Chiswick High
Road, London W4 (01-995 0345).

**British Stock Car Racing Association
(BRISCA):** 232 High Road, Wood Green,
London N22 (01-888 8456).

British Trial and Rally Drivers Association (BT & RDA): D. B. Smith, Hurst
Street, Reddish, Stockport, Cheshire.

Car Grasstrack Racing Organisation:
P. Beaumont, 53 Meadowfield, Sleaford,
Lincolnshire (Lincoln 27193).

Clubmans Register: R. Hall, 4 Barclay
Oval, Woodford Wells, Essex (01-504
0440).

**Federation Internationale de l'Automobile (FIA) and Commission Sportive
Internationale (CSI):** 8 Place de la
Concorde, Paris.

Formula Ford International: N. Brittan,
35 Alwyne Road, London N1 (01-359
0755).

Formula Vee Association: Volkswagen
House, Brighton Road, Purley, Surrey
CR2 2UQ (01-668 4100).

**Jim Russell International Racing Drivers
School:** Snetterton Circuit, Norwich
NOR 10X (Quidenham 451); and at
Mallory Park Circuit, Kirkby Mallory,
Leicester (Earl Shilton 2841).

Karting Magazine: Bank House, Susan
Wood, Chislehurst, Kent (01-467 6533).

Kentish Border Car Club: B. Wright, 145
High Street, Orpington, Kent BR6 0IQ
(Orpington 23777).

**Lancashire and Cheshire Jalopy Racing
Club:** C. Taylor, Ivy Cottage, Lower
Whitley, Near Warrington, Lancashire.

Lincoln Motor Cycle and Car Club: J.
Timms, 10 Coningsby Crescent, Bracebridge Heath, Lincoln (Lincoln 28801).

Liverpool Motor Club: D. Aukland, 6
Hard Lane, St Helens, Lancashire (St
Helens 27703).

Mini Seven Club: M. Burton, 'Moonrakers', Great Coxwell, Near Faringdon,
Berkshire (Faringdon 2029).

Monoposto Racing Club: M. Cowburn, 27
Van Dyke Close, Putney Heath Lane,
London SW15.

Motor Circuit Developments Limited:
Brands Hatch, Fawkham, Near Dartford, Kent (West Ash 331).

Motor Racing Stables Limited: Brands
Hatch, Fawkham, Near Dartford, Kent
(West Ash 404/488); and at Silverstone
Circuit, Silverstone, Near Towcester,
Northants (Silverstone 271).

Northern Car Track Racing Organisation: E. Ganderton, 114 The Garland,
Clifton, York.

**Royal Automobile Club (Motor Sport
Division):** 31 Belgrave Square, London
SW1 (01-235 8601).

750 Motor Club: D. Bradley, 'Zolder', 16
Woodstock Road, Witney, Oxon
(Witney 2285).

Spedeworth: Aldershot Stadium, Tongham, Near Farnham, Surrey (Aldershot
20182).

Thames Estuary Automobile Club (TEAC):
P. E. Austin, 65 St Andrews Road,
Shoeburyness, Essex (Shoeburyness
2418).

Thruxton Saloon Car Racing School:
Thruxton Circuit, Near Andover, Hants
(Weyhill 607).

Vintage Sports Car Club (VSCC): Bone
Lane, (Off Mill Lane), Newbury, Berks
(Newbury 4411).

Weston-super-Mare Motor Club: Mrs C.
Smith, Rook Hayes, Kewstoke Road,
Kewstoke, Weston-super-Mare, Somerset
(Weston-super-Mare 29942).